SHORT AND SWEET

WITH A TREAT

52 Already Done, Ready-for-fun Family Home Evenings

Includes CD-ROM to Instantly Print

Activities in Color or Black and White

Each Activity Teaches a *Gospel Standard*

Introducing the Author and Illustrator,

Creators of the Following Series of Books and Printable CD-ROM Versions of Each Book:

- **PRIMARY LESSON ACTIVITIES & HANDOUTS** (for Manuals 1-7 & *Faith in God Activity Days*): *Primary Partners: Nursery-Age 3 Sunbeams*, Vol. 1 and Vol. 2 and *Happy Handouts: Lesson Ideas and Coloring Pages*, *CTR-A* and *CTR-B* (ages 4-7); *Book of Mormon, D&C, New Testament*, and *Old Testament* (ages 8-11); *Faith-in-God: We Love Activity Days* and *Super Activity Days and Socials* (girls 8-11)
- **CURRENT SHARING TIME:** *Sharing Time, Sharing Time Treasures,* and *Singing Fun*
- **GAMES & ACTIVITIES FOR FAMILY HOME EVENING & PRIMARY** (colored & ready-to-use):
  - **Activities Series:** *Gospel Fun Activities, Fun in a Flash, Tons of Fun, Jesus Loves Me*
  - **Games Series:** *Gospel Games* and *Funner Than Fun Gospel Games*
- **SINGING** (colored & ready-to-use) Series: *Super Little Singers* and *Super Singing Activities*
- **YOUNG WOMEN Series:** *Young Women Fun-tastic! Activities: Lesson Lifesavers* for manuals 1-3 and *Young Women Fun-tastic! Personal Progress Motivators*

Mary Ross, Author   Jennette Guymon-King, Illustrator

Printed in United States of America
First Printing: March 2008

Short and Sweet with a Treat: 52 Already Done, Ready-for-Fun Family Home Evenings

ISBN 10: 1-59811-505-7

ISBN 13: 978-1-59811-505-5

Short and Sweet with a Treat
INTRODUCTION

Here are 52 weeks' worth of short and sweet family home evenings to create and present in a flash by printing the games and activities from the enclosed CD-ROM in color or black-and-white. They're already done and ready for fun!

The themes in each lesson are suitable for all ages, but the activities presented are designed to be most enjoyable for young Primary-age children. To maximize fun and learning for your family, you will want to tailor each lesson (including the activity) to best fit your children's ages, interests, and abilities.

Each lesson and activity focuses on a *Gospel Standard* found in the *Faith in God* booklet. With each lesson you will find coordinating songs, a scripture, a short lesson, a print-and-use activity, a challenge, and a treat.

Simply print the activity visuals from CD-ROM by inserting the enclosed CD into your computer and opening the CD directory to the designated image codes found in each lesson.

For example, in lesson 1, for the *Octopus FHE Chart* (shown), select either the black and white images 1a, 1b, and 1c, or the color images 1aC, 1bC, and 1cC. Select them one at a time and then print. If you see, e.g., 30aC1 and 30aC2, you will know the second color choice is to print faces of children in different ethnic groups. Also in lesson #1 you may print a prayer elevator (shown) to remind you to have family prayer each day.

Additional Helps: (1) See *Singing Meter* in lesson 40 to motivate singing. (2) Access articles, lessons, and music at the Church website (www.lds.org Gospel Library, then click on "magazines," "lessons," "music"). You can find the accompaniment for most songs, so a piano isn't necessary. Enjoy!

TABLE OF CONTENTS

SHORT AND SWEET
52 Already Done, Ready-for-Fun Family Home Evenings

Introduction i

1. Family Night and Family Prayer 1-2
2. My Gospel Standards Overview 3-4

FOLLOW HEAVENLY FATHER'S PLAN

3. Heaven Sent and Heaven Bound 5-6
4. I Am a Child of God 7-8
5. The Gospel Is Our Road Map Back to Heaven 9-10
6. Heavenly Father's Plan 11-12

REMEMBER BAPTISMAL COVENANT & LISTEN TO HOLY GHOST

7. Special Baptism Promises 13-14
8. Invite the Holy Ghost 15-16
9. The Spirit of Truth 17-18
10. The Holy Ghost, Our Guide 19-20

CHOOSE THE RIGHT; I KNOW I CAN REPENT

11. Following Jesus 21-22
12. Choosing the Right 23-24
13. Repent and Live the Gospel 25-26
14. Choices and Consequences 27-28
15. Be Strong Against Temptation 29-30

I am HAPPY when I am HONEST.

BE HONEST WITH HEAVENLY FATHER, OTHERS, & MYSELF

16. Happy When Honest 31-32

17. Telling the Truth 33-34

18. Honest in Thought, Word, and Deed 35-36

19. Honest Tithes 37-38

USE NAMES OF HEAVENLY FATHER & JESUS CHRIST REVERENTLY; DON'T SWEAR OR USE CRUDE WORDS

20. Reverence the Names of God the Father

and the Son 39-40

21. Show Respect 41-42

CHOOSE SABBATH ACTIVITIES THAT WILL HELP ME FEEL CLOSE TO HEAVENLY FATHER & JESUS CHRIST

22. Righteous Sabbath Activities 43-44

23. Sweet Sabbath Day 45-46

24. Search and Ponder Scriptures 47-48

HONOR MY PARENTS & STRENGTHEN MY FAMILY

25. Strengthen Family 49-50

26. Communicate with Family 51-52

27. Get to Know Extended Family . . . 53-54

28. Harmony at Home 55-56

29. Sharing Work 57-58

KEEP MIND & BODY SACRED AND PURE

30. Pure Thoughts 59-60
31. Tune into Righteous Thoughts 61-62
32. Accountable W.O.W. Actions 63-64
33. Word of Wisdom 65-66

DRESS MODESTLY TO SHOW RESPECT FOR HEAVENLY FATHER & MYSELF

34. Neat & Modest Appearance 67-68
35. Dress Modestly to Stay Chaste 69-70

READ & WATCH THINGS THAT ARE PLEASING TO HEAVENLY FATHER

36. Praiseworthy Entertainment 71-72
37. Scripture Blessings 73-74
38. "Bee" Smart Reading Choices 75-76

LISTEN TO MUSIC THAT IS PLEASING TO HEAVENLY FATHER

39. "Note"worthy Songs 77-78
40. Uplifting Music and Songs 79-80
41. Hum Righteous Thoughts 81-82

SEEK GOOD FRIENDS & TREAT OTHERS KINDLY

42. Love Others 83-84

43. Serve Others 85-86

44. Joy in Service 87-88

45. Show Loving Care 89-90

46. Say "No" to Peer Pressure 91-92

47. Forgive Others 93-94

48. Prepare to Share the Gospel 95-96

LIVE WORTHY TO GO TO THE TEMPLE &
DO MY PART TO HAVE AN ETERNAL FAMILY

49. Gain Eternal Life 97-98

50. Families Can Be Together Forever 99-100

51. Prepare for the Temple 101-102

52. Eternal Marriage & Families 103-104

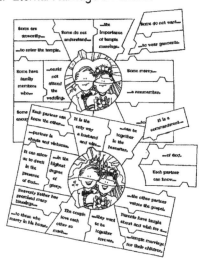

#1
FAMILY NIGHT & FAMILY PRAYER

AHEAD OF TIME: Print images* (shown) using CD-ROM—codes for the *Octopus FHE Chart:* 01a, 01b, and 01c (b&w), or 01aC, 01bC, and 01cC (color); the *Elevator Prayer Chart* (print a set for each child): 01d (b&w), 01dC1 and 01dC2 (color).

To make: (1) *FHE Chart*—cut out images, glue legs on octopus, write family names on hearts, and glue magnets on back of octopus and hearts to mount on refrigerator. (2) *Prayer Chart*—cut out and glue boy or girl head on wordstrip, cut slits in top and bottom of elevator, thread strip through, and tape wordstrip ends together where indicated so wordstrip strip will move freely.

SONGS & SCRIPTURE

Sing "Family Prayer" and "Family Night" (*Children's Songbook,* 189, 195); read Deuteronomy 11:19.

SHORT LESSON

Draw your family close as you have family home evening each week and daily family prayer. Both of these activities help spiritually strengthen family members and can help our testimonies grow.

Having family home evening helps bring families closer as you learn about Heavenly Father's plan and learn to choose the right and withstand the temptations of the world. It helps families learn love and service.

President Hinckley teaches that we will feel "peace and joy" as we pray as a family (see *Teachings of Gordon B. Hinckley,* 216). Family prayer confirms the truth of the gospel to our soul. It helps to invite the Holy Ghost to guide, bless, direct, and provide spiritual protection. It can increase family love. Someone said, "The family that prays together stays together."

Elder Robert D. Hales has suggested that we can be blessed immeasurably as we hold family councils and spend time showing sincere interest in the lives of family members (see "With All the Feeling of a Tender Parent: A Message of Hope to Families," *Ensign,* May 2004).

See also Carol B. Thomas, "Strengthen Home & Family," *Ensign*, May 2002; James E. Faust, "Enriching Our Lives through Family Home Evening," *Ensign*, Feb. 1991; Gordon B. Hinckley, "The Blessings of Family Prayer," *Ensign*, June 2003.

ACTIVITIES

1. Assign family home evening responsibilities by placing family-named hearts next to the responsibilities on the *Octopus FHE Chart* (shown).

2. Give children an *Elevator Prayer Chart* (shown) to remind them to have individual and family prayers daily. Move face-arrow to first day, then down to reveal message at the end of the week.

CHALLENGE

Talk about ways to improve family home evening and family prayer.

TREATS

Sunday-to-Saturday Mints. Give each family member seven small butter mints one at a time. As each mint melts in their mouth, have them say the days of the week. Then say, "Heavenly Father and Jesus "mint" [meant] for us to have family prayer every day, Sunday through Saturday." Then give them another mint to remind them to have FHE each week.

MORE LESSON IDEAS: See *Primary CTR-B Manual 3*, lesson 34.

#2 ✓
MY GOSPEL STANDARDS OVERVIEW

AHEAD OF TIME: Print *My Gospel Standards Cross-Match Puzzle** (shown) using CD-ROM—codes: 02 (b&w) or 02C (color).

SONGS & SCRIPTURE

Sing "Nephi's Courage" and "I Will Follow God's Plan for Me" (*Children's Songbook*, 120, 164); read D&C 59:23.

SHORT LESSON

Heavenly Father has given us *Gospel Standards*, to guide us as we journey through earth life. They are found in the *Faith in God Program* guidebooks (highlighted in activity, right). By living the *Gospel Standards* we can:

1. Chart our course back to heaven and move in that direction by our faithful actions (Alma 7:19). In James 1:22, we learn to be "doers of the word, and not hearers only."
2. Choose the right, combating the evils of the world. EVIL spelled backwards is LIVE. If we live the *Gospel Standards* we can say "no" to temptation (Matthew 6:13).
3. Find peace and comfort to help us rest from our troubles and fears (John 14:27).
4. Be a light (good example), walking in Jesus' footsteps (Matthew 5:16).
5. Serve to build up the kingdom of God on the earth (Moses 1:39).
6. Learn to work and be a missionary (Moroni 9:6).
7. Have the Holy Ghost to guide us (D&C 45:57).

Talk about a blessing that comes from obeying each standard (e.g., when we're honest we feel peace; seeking good friends brings happiness.)

3

*ACTIVITY

To learn the *Gospel Standards,* complete the *Cross-Match Puzzle* by matching the first column lines with the second column lines, writing the number in the center circle. *Example:* The answer for the first line in the left column is "7," as it matches with #7 in the second column. It reads, "I will remember my baptismal covenant and" . . . "listen to the Holy Ghost." Check the answers when complete (as shown).

MY GOSPEL STANDARDS

Find the complete Gospel Standards sentence. Match the first column lines with the second and write your answer in the center circle.

I will remember my baptismal covenant and...	(7)	1 ...treat others kindly.
I will be honest with...	(11)	2 ...pleasing to Heavenly Father.
I will seek good friends and...	(1)	3 ...reverently. I will not swear or use crude words.
I will dress modestly to show respect for...	(9)	4 ...harmful.
I will only read and watch things that are...	(8)	5 ...body sacred and pure.
I will only listen to music that is...	(2)	6 ...repent when I make a mistake.
I will use the names of Heavenly Father and Jesus Christ...	(3)	7 ...listen to the Holy Ghost.
I will keep my mind and...	(5)	8 ...pleasing to Heavenly Father.
I will not partake of things that are...	(4)	9 ...Heavenly Father and myself.
I will do those things on the Sabbath that will...	(13)	10 ...the temple.
I will choose the right. I know I can...	(6)	11 ...Heavenly Father, others, and myself.
I will live now to be worthy to go to...	(10)	12 ...plan for me.
I will follow Heavenly Father's...	(12)	13 ...help me feel close to Heavenly Father.

CHALLENGE

Each week try living a different *Gospel Standard.* Write it on a card, pray about it, and record your inspiration. Then share your ideas with the family.

TREATS

"Let"tuce Live Gospel Standards Salad. Place the family's favorite fruity salad (e.g., cottage cheese and fruit, or Jell-O with whipping cream) on top of a lettuce leaf. As you eat, say, "'Let'tuce live the *Gospel Standards* each day and harvest a garden full of blessings."

MORE LESSON IDEAS: See *Primary Old Testament Manual 6,* lesson 47.

#3
HEAVEN SENT & HEAVEN BOUND

> **AHEAD OF TIME:** Print *Premortal Life/Earth Life Quiz** (shown) using CD-ROM—codes: 03 (b&w), or 03C1 or 03C2 (color). To make, cut out images and plastic "spirits" as follows: using a clear poly/vinyl sheet protector, cut out dolls with head on fold line (with two sides to slip over doll to show how spirit enters and leaves the body).

SONGS & SCRIPTURE

Sing "I Lived in Heaven" and "I Will Follow God's Plan" (*Children's Songbook*, 4, 164); read D&C 58:28.

SHORT LESSON

We are heaven sent and can be heaven bound. Heavenly Father has a special plan for us to come to earth and be tested (Abraham 3:25). We heard about this plan while we lived in heaven, and we shouted for joy at the good news.

If we live all of His commandments and trust in Jesus Christ, our Savior and Redeemer, we can return to heaven. Jesus died for us, making it possible for all mankind to be resurrected. He suffered for our sins so that we can repent. If we exercise our faith in Him by being repentant and obedient, we can pass the tests of life and return to Heavenly Father and Jesus someday. (See Henry B. Eyring, "Spiritual Preparedness: Start Early & Be Steady," *Ensign*, Nov. 2005; Robert D. Hales, "To Act for Ourselves: The Gift & Blessings of Agency," *Ensign*, May 2006.)

*ACTIVITY

Show images (right) to answer questions:

Where did we come from? (Show *Premortal Life* circle.) Long before we were born, we lived with Heavenly Father and Jesus Christ in our first estate (heaven). We lived there as spirits without a body (show plastic spirit). There we passed a test in order to come to earth and receive a physical body.

What test did we pass to come to earth? While we were in heaven, we chose to follow Jesus and keep all of Heavenly Father's commandments.

Let's write in the *Premortal Life* circle what we did. We passed the first test, so we were sent to earth.

(Place plastic spirit over body on *Earth* circle.) Our spirit was given a chance to come to earth to live in a body to prove ourselves.

What do we need to do to pass the earth life test? Here on earth we have a second chance to prove ourselves, to live all of Heavenly Father's commandments. Under Heavenly Father's direction, Jesus created this beautiful earth for us to live on with a body, so we can be tested. If we keep the commandments we will have passed the test and can receive our reward. In Abraham 3:26 we read, "and they who keep their second estate shall have glory added upon their heads for ever and ever." The decisions we make will help us to return to live with Heavenly Father and Jesus. (In the second estate *Earth* circle, shown, write what you will do.)

CHALLENGE

Talk about what we can do to keep Heavenly Father's commandments so we can return to live with Him someday.

TREATS

Heaven and Earth Cookie or Pudding Painting. Frost a cookie with white frosting (heaven cloud) and chocolate frosting (earth). Or fingerpaint a cloud with white pudding, and earth with chocolate pudding onto paper. As you eat each section, consider your decisions in each place.

MORE LESSON IDEAS: See *Primary D&C Manual 5,* lesson 28.

#4
I AM A CHILD OF GOD

> *AHEAD OF TIME:* Print *Child of God Paper Dolls and Clothing** (shown) using CD-ROM—codes: 1. *girl paper doll:* 04a (b&w) or 04aC1 or 4aC2 (color); 2. *boy paper doll:* 04b (b&w) or 04bC1 or 04bC2 (color).

SONGS & SCRIPTURE

Sing "I Am a Child of God," and "I Lived in Heaven," in *Children's Songbook* (4, 6) and read Psalm 82:6.

SHORT LESSON

We are all of great worth and value, according to our Father in Heaven, who knows us perfectly. We can all say, "I am a child of God." This is how we know (now would be a good time to introduce the *Child of God Paper Dolls* (see "Activity" on next page):

1. We are the spirit children of Heavenly Parents. They created our spirit. We first lived with Them in heaven as spirits. We were taught Heavenly Father's plan of happiness. We are on the earth now, and when we learn His plan, our spirit can tell us it is true. (Place pants on *Dolls.*)

2. Heavenly Father and Jesus created our body of flesh and bones in Their image (Moses 2:27). This way we could come to earth and learn to make right choices. We can learn Heavenly Father's plan and learn to be like Jesus (John 13:15).

3. Heavenly Father and His Son Jesus Christ created us so that we can become like Them someday and have the happiness They have.

4. Heavenly Father's plan of happiness is the gospel of Jesus Christ. When we attend church, read our scriptures, and have family home evening, we can learn to live like Heavenly Father and Jesus.

5. Heavenly Father sent His Only Begotten Son, Jesus Christ, to the earth to show us how to live His plan (3 Nephi 27:21).

7

6. They gave us the Spirit of God (the Holy Ghost) to guide us.
7. We can pray to Heavenly Father and He will listen to us and answer our prayers.
8. They know us and love each of us (Luke 12:6-7). They know our every thought, word, need, and deed (Alma 18:32). (Place shirts on *Dolls.*)
9. We can become like Heavenly Father. As we live His commandments we can move toward perfection and be like Him someday.
10. We can prepare by following Jesus and the prophets (2 Nephi 31:10). If we choose the right each day we can live with Them again someday, and have eternal life (D&C 14:7).

*ACTIVITY

Cut out *Child of God Paper Dolls* and clothing (shown) and talk about the lesson points 1 through 10 above.

CHALLENGE

We can show that we want to become like Heavenly Father by asking, "What would Jesus do?" before each action, then following Jesus to live Heavenly Father's plan.

TREATS

Gingerbread (or Sugar Cookie) Boy or Girl. While eating, talk about some of the ways Heavenly Father shows His love for His children.

MORE LESSON IDEAS: See *Primary Nursery Manual 1*, lesson 1.

#5

THE GOSPEL IS OUR ROAD MAP BACK TO HEAVEN

AHEAD OF TIME: Print the *Right Road to Heaven Road Map* and *Trusty Truck** (shown) using CD-ROM—codes: 05 (b&w) or 05C (color). To make, cut out truck and cut around border of map.

SONGS & SCRIPTURE

Sing "I Lived in Heaven" and "Families Can Be Together Forever" (*Children's Songbook*, 4, 188); read Moses 1:39.

SHORT LESSON

We came to earth to be tested, to learn of Heavenly Father's plan, and to choose the right so that we can be found worthy to return to Heavenly Father again.

Heavenly Father wants us to have a good experience while we are here. There are many right choices to be made along the way. Elder James M. Paramore once suggested that the road is clearly marked by Heavenly Father but that we might be deceived by the ways of the world (see "The Heart and a Willing Mind," *Ensign,* May 1998).

What is the right road to heaven? Now that we are here on earth, we can learn the course Heavenly Father wants us to take. We were not sent here without a map to guide us back home. We are given the gospel of Jesus Christ, the map that leads us to exaltation (life with Heavenly Father and Jesus).

Jesus has provided a road map to heaven with His teachings of the gospel and with His example. The more we learn about Jesus' teachings and Heavenly Father's plan for us, the easier it will be to find the right path and stay on it to find our way back to our heavenly home. We can stay on the strait and narrow path by attending church, reading the scriptures, following the prophet, and keeping the commandments.

9

We will know what to do along the way if we are worthy of inspiration and if we pray and seek Heavenly Father's help. The Holy Ghost is also sent to guide us along the way.

*ACTIVITY

Use this *Right Road to Heaven Road Map* (shown) to practice moving through life. Move the truck to show Heavenly Father you can be trusted to make the right choices. Have each choice in your mind as you travel through life, mentally moving your own *Trusty Truck* (you) back to heaven. The road signs show the way back to Heavenly Father. Have children and teens add choices (destinations and roadblocks) they may face on the map.

CHALLENGE

Every day as you pray, think about how you are doing and where you are on the road to heaven. If you get off the path by not choosing the right, you can repent and get back on. Move your *Trusty Truck* (yourself) to choices that show your obedience to God's command-ments. When you partake of the sacrament each week—remembering Jesus and promising to obey the commandments—Heavenly Father will bless and inspire you. He will help you stay on the strait and narrow path that leads back to heaven (2 Nephi 31:18).

TREATS

Trusty Truck Wheels. Round wheel-shaped hard candies. Family can have a "wheelie" good time eating and thinking how sweet it would be to live with Heavenly Father and Jesus again.

MORE LESSON IDEAS: See *Primary CTR-B Manual 3,* lesson 2.

10

#6
HEAVENLY FATHER'S PLAN

> *AHEAD OF TIME:* Print *Plan of Salvation Storyboard* images & wordstrips* using CD-ROM—codes: 06a and 06b (b&w), or 06aC and 06bC (color).

SONGS & SCRIPTURE

Sing "I Am a Child of God" and "I Lived in Heaven" (*Children's Songbook*, 2, 4); read D&C 76:92.

*SHORT LESSON

(Show the *Storyboard* images for each stage of the plan of salvation in the lesson. Lay out each image in a logical order as you go.) *What Is Heavenly Father's Plan of Salvation?*

1. *PREMORTAL LIFE:* Where did we come from? Spencer W. Kimball said that all of our spirits existed "long before this world was created" (*The Teachings of Spencer W. Kimball*, 30). We call this existence heaven. In heaven, Jesus and Heavenly Father lived with us, and we had our first lessons there (D&C 138:56).

2. *BIRTH:* Heavenly Father wanted us to receive a physical body, to learn to choose between right and wrong and have the chance to be like Him. We chose to follow this plan, so we were sent to earth (Job 38:4, 7). When we were born, we forgot what happened before, so we could be tested (Abraham 3:5).

3. *EARTH:* On earth we must live by faith in Heavenly Father and Jesus. As we study the scriptures, pray, and listen to the prophet and the Holy Ghost, our faith increases. We are born to earthly parents, yet we are all children of God our Heavenly Father (the father of our spirits—Romans 8:16). If we keep the commandments we will be blessed (Abraham 3:26).

4. *DEATH & SPIRIT WORLD:* When we are righteous and we die, our spirits go to the spirit world, where God takes care of us and we see our loved ones" (Ecclesiastes 12:7).

5. *RESURRECTION:* Because of Jesus' Atonement, we can be resurrected with a perfect body (2 Nephi 9:13; 1 Corinthians 15:22, Alma 11:43–44). Everyone can be resurrected. If we are worthy, we can also live with Heavenly Father and Jesus in the highest kingdom, the celestial kingdom (D&C 76: 51–53; 92–94).

In the celestial kingdom we can be like God (D&C 76:95) and live with our families forever.

To live there we must first have faith in Jesus Christ, repent, be baptized, receive the Holy Ghost, and go to the temple. We must prove we can keep all of Heavenly Father's commandments. If we make a wrong choice we must repent and not do it again, so we can one day be like Heavenly Father and Jesus Christ.

Read about those who will live in the other two kingdoms: the terrestrial kingdom (D&C 76:71–79) and the telestial kingdom (D&C 76:81, 101–3).

ACTIVITY—Plan of Salvation Quiz

Use the *Storyboard* images (shown above) laid out on the table/floor. Randomly lay the wordstrips (outlined below) facedown. Draw a wordstrip and decide where it goes, placing it under the appropriate *Storyboard* stage(s) of life (some may go in several). *Quiz wordstrips:*   *Answers:*

Quiz wordstrips	Answers
• Live with Heavenly Father and Jesus	Premortal life, celestial kingdom
• Be with our family	Premortal life, earth life, celestial kingdom
• Have the scriptures to guide us	Earth life
• Have only a spirit body	Premortal life, spirit world
• Have a physical body	Earth life, all three kingdoms
• Learn about Heavenly Father's plan	Premortal, earth life, spirit world
• Experience hard work, sorrow, and death	Earth life
• Be able to have children	Earth life, celestial kingdom

CHALLENGE

Review the plan of salvation and goals needed to reach the celestial kingdom.

TREATS

Celestial Smile Cookies. Frost a yellow smile on a round sugar cookie to remind us that happy smiles are on their way as we dream about living in the celestial kingdom with Heavenly Father and Jesus.

MORE LESSON IDEAS: See *Primary Old Testament Manual 6,* lesson 1.

#7
SPECIAL BAPTISM PROMISES

> ***AHEAD OF TIME:*** Print *Promises Two-Sided Puzzle* * (shown) using CD-ROM—codes: 07 (b&w) or 07C (color). To make, fold puzzle and glue back-to-back, covering the entire puzzle. Then cut out on the lines to create the two-sided sign and wordstrips.

SONGS & SCRIPTURE

Sing "When Jesus Christ Was Baptized" and "When I Am Baptized" (*Children's Songbook,* 102, 103); read 3 Nephi 11:33.

SHORT LESSON

When we are baptized, we make a covenant (a two-way promise). We make special promises to Heavenly Father, and He makes special promises to us. God will honor the promises He makes to us if we honor our promises to Him. Through these promises, we can obtain exaltation, which is eternal life with Heavenly Father, Jesus Christ, and our families. (See Mosiah 18:7–17 and D&C 20:75–79.)

Let's review the promises we make to Heavenly Father at baptism, which we can renew each week when we partake of the sacrament:

1. To take upon us Christ's name to "stand as witnesses of God" (see Mosiah 18:8–9).
2. To keep Heavenly Father's commandments.
3. To serve the Lord. Jesus was our greatest example as He taught us how to serve. "When ye are in the service of your fellow beings ye are only in the service of your God" (Mosiah 2:17).

Now let's review the wonderful promises Heavenly Father makes to us when we fulfill our baptismal promises to Him:

13

1. To give us the gift of the Holy Ghost. (He wants us to be guided and comforted.)
2. To forgive us when we repent. (He wants us to change our lives so we can be happy like Him.)
3. To let us live with Him forever. (He created the celestial kingdom where we can live with Him forever.)

- to take upon the name of Jesus Christ
- to keep the commandments.
- to serve the Lord.

*ACTIVITY

1. Show the "I Promise" sign. Place under it the promises we make to Heavenly Father when we are baptized. We can review these promises each week when we partake of the sacrament.
2. Turn the sign over to show "Heavenly Father Promises." Place under the sign the promises Heavenly Father makes to us when we are faithful.

CHALLENGE

Brainstorm as a family to name at least one or two ways we can obey each of the baptismal promises discussed in the lesson.

TREATS

Promise Handprint Cookie. Explain to family that we often raise our hand to promise things. To make cookie, roll sugar cookie dough into a ball and flatten. Press a small child's hand in dough to make a handprint, then sprinkle colored sugar in handprint. (To make colored sugar, put sugar and food coloring in a bottle, then shake.) Instead of using colored sugar, you may paint handprint impression with cookie paint. (To make cookie paint, mix two teaspoons canned milk with food coloring.)
Bake cookie at 350°F for 8–10 minutes.

MORE LESSON IDEAS: See *Primary CTR-B Manual 3, lesson* 13.

#8
INVITE THE HOLY GHOST

AHEAD OF TIME: Print *Invites the Spirit Game* bag label and wordstrips*(shown) using CD-ROM—codes: 08 (b&w), or 08C (color). To make, cut out images and place in bag.

SONGS & SCRIPTURE

Sing "Listen, Listen" and "Seek the Lord Early" (*Children's Songbook*,107, 108); read D&C 88:3.

SHORT LESSON

Why do we need the Holy Ghost to guide us?

1. He is a member of the Godhead who brings messages to us from Heavenly Father and Jesus (D&C 14:8).
2. He comforts us, filling us with "hope and perfect love" (Moroni 8:26).
3. He brings clarity to our minds so that we can tell the difference between right and wrong, true and false (see James E. Faust, "The Devil's Throat," *Ensign,* May 2003).
4. He helps us "know the truth of all things" (Moroni 10:4–5). The voice of the Lord speaks to us through the Spirit by letting our hearts feel the truth of what our minds are learning (see M. Russell Ballard, "Marvelous Are the Revelations of the Lord," *Ensign,* May 1998).

The Holy Ghost helps us in many other ways if we invite Him. The Spirit can direct and instruct us, as well as provide spiritual protection while we are here on earth.

We can invite the Spirit through:

1. Personal and family prayer (D&C 90:24).
2. Studying the scriptures (2 Nephi 32:3).
3. Obedience (1 Nephi 3:7—Nephi did as the Lord commanded).
4. Service (Mosiah 2:11—King Benjamin served his people).

15

5. Avoiding temptation. As we avoid the sinful things of the world, the Holy Ghost can draw near to us (see David A. Bednar, "That We May Always Have His Spirit to Be with Us," *Ensign,* May 2006).

ACTIVITY:

We should pray often, and when we pray, we should ask for the Spirit to guide us to make right choices. Let's learn choices that invite the Holy Ghost by playing the *Invites the Spirit Game.*

To Play: Divide into two teams. Take turns drawing a choice wordstrip from the bag and reading it aloud. The player makes a choice by turning the "face" bag around to vote either "Invites the Spirit" or "Turns the Spirit Away." Each correct response is worth 1 point. Play 10–15 minutes or until all wordstrips are read.

CHALLENGE:

When we have the Spirit of God in our home, we are blessed (see Robert D. Hales, "With All the Feeling of a Tender Parent: A Message of Hope to Families," *Ensign,* May 2004). Think about the actions that invite the Spirit or turn the Spirit away. Talk about what you can do to invite the Spirit into your home. Review the list (shown left) of things we can do to invite the Spirit.

TREATS:

Smiley-Frowny Cookie. On the same side of a round sugar cookie, frost a smile at the top and a frown at the bottom, with two eyes in the middle. Tell family that when we do things that invite the Spirit we can turn our frown upside down.

MORE LESSON IDEAS: See *Primary D&C Manual 5,* lesson 7.

#9

THE SPIRIT OF TRUTH

> **AHEAD OF TIME:** Print *Spirit of Truth Cross-Match Puzzle**
> (shown) using CD-ROM—codes: 09 (b&w) and 09C (color).

SONGS & SCRIPTURE

Sing "The Still Small Voice" and "Search, Ponder, and Pray" (*Children's Songbook*, 106, 109); read Mosiah 5:2.

SHORT LESSON

If we remember our baptism promises and keep Heavenly Father's commandments, we are promised that we can have the third member of the Godhead, the Holy Ghost, to guide us.

His Spirit is the Spirit of Truth. If we do not obey the commandments, another spirit can speak to us that is not from God (the spirit of lies—Moses 4:4). As we live the commandments we can be worthy of the Holy Spirit. In John 16:13 we learn, "Howbeit when he, the Spirit of truth, is come, he will guide you into all truth."

Elder Joseph B. Wirthlin explained that the Holy Ghost is a revelator, revealing the word of God to us. The Holy Ghost tells us that the gospel is true, and He helps us gain a testimony that Jesus lives. He guides our choices and helps us find truth (see *Finding Peace in Our Lives*, 41).

*ACTIVITY

How can you tell it is the Holy Ghost? Show the *Spirit of Truth Cross-Match* (shown) to learn the difference between righteous ideas (ideas from God) and unrighteous ideas (ideas not from God). Ideas can be compared to a light going on inside our mind. The light that comes from God is a bright light that brings a warm, happy feeling. The light that does not come from God is a dim light that brings a cold, sad feeling.

To do the *Cross-Match*, draw a line from each box to the lightbulb where it belongs.

17

ANSWERS AND ADDITIONAL SCRIPTURES

Ideas from God: Warm feeling inside (D&C 9:8). You want to do good; you want to love and serve God (Moroni 7:13). You have peace in your mind (D&C 6:23 and John 14:27).

Ideas not from God: Confusion (D&C 9:9). You want to do wrong; you do not want to follow Jesus Christ; you doubt Him (Moroni 7:17).

CHALLENGE

Memorize Moroni 10:4–5 to learn that truth comes from the

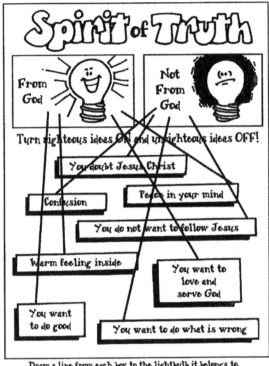

Draw a line from each box to the lightbulb it belongs to.

Holy Ghost. This is known as the Book of Mormon promise, telling us that the Spirit will guide us to not only know the truthfulness of the Book of Mormon, but help us in all aspects of our lives to know what is right and true. Remember, this knowledge is based on our faith and obedience. Also read,"Words of the Prophet: The Gift of the Holy Ghost," by President Gordon B. Hinckley, *New Era,* January 2005, 5 (see You Are Not Alone).

TREATS

Clutter & Clutter-free Cookies. Frost two cookies, one cluttered with paper confetti and the other simply decorated. Talk of keeping our lives free from the clutter of the world and our mind open to listening to the Holy Ghost. This way He knows we are ready and seeking inspiration. Serve additional clutter-free cookies.

MORE LESSON IDEAS: See *Primary Old Testament Manual 6,* lesson 27.

#10

THE HOLY GHOST, OUR GUIDE

AHEAD OF TIME: Print *Light of the Holy Ghost Mobile** (shown) using CD-ROM—codes: 10 (b&w) or 10 C (color). To make, cut out and glue lightbulbs back to back. Punch a hole at the top. Tie a 12-inch ribbon at the top to hang.

SONGS & SCRIPTURE

Sing "The Still Small Voice" and "Teach Me to Walk in the Light" (*Children's Songbook,* 106, 177); read D&C 8:2.

SHORT LESSON

We are given the gift of the Holy Ghost after baptism. The Holy Ghost, often called the Holy Spirit or the Spirit of God, is a member of the Godhead with Heavenly Father and Jesus Christ. If we are worthy, the Holy Ghost can guide us throughout our life.

Six Things We Can Do to Be Worthy of the Holy Ghost (on *Mobile*):

1. *Repent.* Read 3 Nephi 27:20 (stand spotless . . . at last day).
2. *Obey Commandments.* Read James 2:17 (faith without works is dead).
3. *Pray.* Ask for the companionship of the Holy Ghost.
4. *Ask Righteously in Faith.* Read Enos 1:15 and discuss what kinds of things we can ask for (righteous desires).
5. *Forsake Worldly Things.* Read 3 Nephi 12:30 and talk about things of the world we should not participate in.
6. *Be Baptized and Honor Covenants.* If we honor our covenants we place ourselves on the path to eternal life. Baptism is the gate that leads to the strait and narrow path. Rely on Jesus Christ to help you stay on the path. Learn of Him, follow Him, and testify of Him. Read about the path, the gate, the Holy Ghost, and a promise in 2 Nephi 31:18–20.

   To have the constant companionship of the Holy Spirit is one of the greatest blessings we can have.

Six Things the Holy Ghost Does If We Are Worthy (opposite side of *Mobile*):

1. *Teaches and directs.* He helps keep us on the strait and narrow path leading to heaven (2 Nephi 32:5).
2. *Shows Us Things to Come.* He guides us into truth and shows us things to come (John 16:13).
3. *Manifests Truth.* Gives us perfect knowledge (Moroni 7:16).
4. *Bears Record.* The Holy Ghost bears record of the Father and the Son (Moroni 10:4–5).
5. *Comforts.* He teaches us peaceable things (D&C 36:2).
6. *Reveals Things to Our Heart and Mind.* Elder Henry B. Eyring explained that we truly can hear the still, small voice of the Holy Ghost when we humble ourselves and let our mind and heart be calm and peaceful (see "As a Child," *Ensign*, May 2006).

*ACTIVITY

Fill in missing words on *Mobile* (shown) by looking up the scriptures.

CHALLENGE

Talk about ways having the Holy Ghost guides you (e.g., helps you not feel scared, helps you learn something hard at school, shows you which choice is right, etc.).

TREATS

Worthy M&Ms. With a large bowl of M&Ms (or other small candies) set in front of you, brainstorm actions that will help you be worthy of the companionship of the Holy Ghost. Play in teams of two or more. For two minutes, team members call out actions that will allow the Holy Ghost to guide them. Each team collects a piece of candy for each action named. The team with the most candies over all takes the remaining candies in the bowl.

MORE LESSON IDEAS: See *Young Women Manual 1,* lesson 4.

#11
FOLLOWING JESUS

> **AHEAD OF TIME:** Print *Faithful Footsteps Flip Chart* * (shown) from
> CD-ROM—codes: 11a, 11b, and 11c (b&w); or 11aC, 11bC, and 11cC
> (color). To make, glue cards together, placing the first, second, third,
> fourth, and fifth chart behind the first so that footsteps show below each
> chart (with *Faithful Footstep Flip Chart* at the top).

SONGS & SCRIPTURE

Sing "Jesus Once Was a Little Child" and "I'm Trying to Be Like Jesus"
(*Children's Songbook*, 55, 78); read 2 Nephi 31:10.

SHORT LESSON

Heavenly Father sent Jesus to the earth to show us how we should live. We can choose the right as Jesus did, but if we make a mistake, Jesus has made it possible for us to repent. Jesus was perfect and was chosen by Heavenly Father to suffer for our sins. This means we can be forgiven when we repent.

We can follow Jesus by learning about His teachings and example. When asked what the greatest commandment was, Jesus answered, "Thou shalt love the Lord thy God with all thy heart, and with all thy soul, and with all thy mind. This is the first and great commandment. And the second is like unto it, Thou shalt love thy neighbour as thyself" (Matthew 22:37–39).

President Ezra Taft Benson said that we shouldn't worry what worldly people around us might do or say. We should stay on the path Christ has shown us, the path that leads to "safety and exaltation" (*The Teachings of Ezra Taft Benson*, 26). Psalms 37 teaches, "The steps of a good man are ordered by the Lord: and he delighteth in his way. . . . The law of his God is in his heart; none of his steps shall slide" (verses 23 and 31).

*ACTIVITY

How can we follow Jesus and live His teachings? Flip through the *Faithful Footsteps Flip Chart* pages (shown) to learn how we can follow in the footsteps of Jesus and endure to the end.

Let's write on each chart things we can do to follow Jesus. Each step brings us closer to eternal life—life with Heavenly Father and Jesus. Read and explain 2 Nephi 31:20. "Press forward" means to walk in the steps of Jesus, to do as He would do. As we press forward, enduring to the end, we will have the greatest of all gifts—eternal life.

CHALLENGE

Think of ideas to write on *Flip Chart* and how you can help your family follow Jesus each day. Ideas: have daily family prayer; bless the food; say individual prayers; gather tithing envelopes for family members to pay tithing; attend tithing settlement as a family; help get house, food, and clothes ready for Sunday on Saturday; attend all your church meetings; get ready quickly on Sunday so you don't make others late; have daily family scripture study; hold weekly family home evening; choose the right to be an example; forgive each other; express love; and serve each other.

TREATS

Footstep Fudge. Talk about following in the footsteps of Jesus. Melt a bag of chocolate chips with one-half can sweetened condensed milk; stir. When fudge is cool, shape with fingers to form feet. Place a small candy (like an M&M) on each toe. Count the toes as you name the five things on the *Faithful Footsteps Flip Chart* that we can do to follow Jesus.

MORE LESSON IDEAS: See *Primary Old Testament Manual 6,* lesson 6.

#12
CHOOSING THE RIGHT

AHEAD OF TIME: Print *CTR Spoons Game* (includes spoons [shown] and situations wordstrips)* using CD-ROM—codes: 12a and 12b (b&w), or 12aC and 12bC (color). To make, cut out spoons, glue a wooden craft stick on back of each, laminate, and cut out again. (Make sure you have one spoon for each player, minus one.) Cut out situations wordstrips and place in a paper bag or other container.

SONGS & SCRIPTURE

Sing "Choose the Right Way" and "I Will Be Valiant" (*Children's Songbook,* 160, 162); read 2 Nephi 10:23.

SHORT LESSON

Happiness comes from choosing the right every day. We have a choice in every situation. We can be valiant and follow the teachings of Jesus and serve in a loving way, or we can make a different choice that we will need to repent of later. But if we are valiant, we will choose the right way and be happy.

We can learn how to choose the right by doing the following:

1. *Have Family Home Evening.* President Thomas S. Monson says the family is the ideal situation for learning, and family home evening helps teach and bring spiritual growth (see "Your Personal Influence," *Ensign,* May 2004).

2. *Attend Church to Learn the Gospel.* President Ezra Taft Benson told members that faithful attendance at Church meetings will bring unique blessings as we learn our gospel responsibilities and perform them diligently (see "To the Young Women of the Church," *Ensign,* Nov. 1986).

3. *Study the Scriptures and Pray for the Holy Ghost to Guide You.* In 1 Nephi 5:21, we learn that the scriptures are good and were preserved for our day so that we can learn God's commandments. Read Moroni 10:4–5 to discover what we can know through study and prayer. Answer the

23

question, How will we know if things are true? (The answer is found in verse 4).

4. *Pray.* You will receive inspiration for your daily choices.

5. *Repent.* Elder Joseph B. Wirthlin assures us that Heavenly Father's plan gives us agency, which allows us to make choices, whether right or wrong. This is how we learn and improve. Jesus suffered for our sins to make it possible for us to repent (see "Deep Roots," *Ensign,* Nov. 1994). This way we can change and take the right path if we make a mistake.

6. *Serve.* You will develop charity, the pure love of Christ (Moroni 4:47).

ACTIVITY

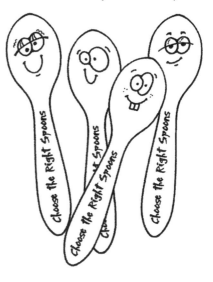

Play the *CTR Spoon Game* to see if you know what to do when you are in a situation where you must make a choice. Learn to choose the right, to do as Jesus would do. Have someone sit the first round out and be the leader. To play, sit in a circle and place spoons in front of you a hand apart. Have one fewer spoons than players. The leader will draw and read a situation and then use his or her imagination to come up with a right or wrong choice to complete it. When a wrong choice is mentioned, players do nothing, and the reader moves on to another situation. When a right choice is made, all players slap their hand on a spoon and grab it. One person will be without a spoon. That person and their spoon are out of the game. The "out" person can draw the next situation and be the leader. Play until the last spoon is grabbed—the one who grabbed it is the winner. Start over and play another round.

CHALLENGE

Brainstorm more situations and play the game again, using your own ideas.

TREATS

CTR Breadsticks. Make breadsticks shaped like C, T, and R. (May use purchased refrigerated bread dough to save time.)

#13

REPENT AND LIVE THE GOSPEL

> **AHEAD OF TIME:** Print *Repentance Word Search Puzzle** (shown) using CD-ROM—codes: 13 (b&w) or 13C (color).

SONGS & SCRIPTURE

Sing "Repentance" and "Help Me, Dear Father" (*Children's Songbook*, 98, 99); read D&C 20:29 and 50:29.

SHORT LESSON

Jesus and Heavenly Father sent us to earth so that we can learn to make good choices. Choosing the right every day is not easy, but if we make a mistake, we can repent. Because Jesus is our elder brother and loves us, He paid the price for our sins by suffering in the Garden of Gethsemane and on the cross. This makes it possible for us to repent. Knowing this, we should try to always make right choices.

Jesus suffered greatly on the cross, but He suffered more in the garden when He prayed for our sins to be forgiven. In Luke 22:44 we read about this suffering: "And being in an agony he prayed more earnestly: and his sweat was as it were great drops of blood falling down to the ground."

All Jesus asks is that we do our best, repent, and follow Him by living His gospel. If we do, we are promised that we will be received in the kingdom of heaven (3 Nephi 9:22).

Because Jesus died on the cross and was resurrected, He made it possible for everyone to be resurrected. Everyone, no matter how they live, will receive a body again after they die, but not everyone will have eternal life. Eternal life is to live with Heavenly Father and Jesus again. We can have this if we repent and live all of the commandments (2 Nephi 31:18).

What does it mean to repent? It means to stop committing the sin, be sorry we did it, and never commit the sin again.

25

The following steps need to be taken to repent: (1) Recognize we have done something wrong. (2) Confess and promise not to do it again. (3) Do all we can to correct what we did wrong, and apologize to those we offended. (4) Pray to Heavenly Father for forgiveness. (5) Promise to live the commandments. (6) Forgive ourselves.

When this process is complete, the Lord will forgive us. He promises that He will "remember them [our sins] no more" (D&C 58:42). But we don't forget our sin. This helps us not to repeat the mistake.

*ACTIVITY

Follow instructions to complete the *Puzzle.*

CHALLENGE

Brainstorm actions that need changing and how you will repent and choose the right. Example: "I said a word that was bad, then said, 'sorry' and found a better word to express my feelings the next time."

TREATS

Repentance Rollups.

Have each person roll out a red fruit rollup as you say, "Jesus rolled out the red carpet for us, giving us the royal treatment when He suffered for our sins. We are God's sons and daughters, princes and princesses in His kingdom. If we repent and follow the strait and narrow path (carpet), we can return to our heavenly home."

MORE LESSON IDEAS: See *Primary New Testament Manual 7*, lesson 30.

#14
CHOICES & CONSEQUENCES

AHEAD OF TIME: Print *Choices & Consequences Match Game** (shown) using CD-ROM—codes: 14a, 14b, and 14c (b&w); or 14aC, 14bC, and 14cC (color). To make, cut out puzzle pieces as shown.

SONGS & SCRIPTURE

Sing "I Will Be Valiant" and "Teach Me to Walk in the Light" (*Children's Songbook,* 162, 177); read 2 Nephi 13:10.

SHORT LESSON

Before coming to this earth we were given the choice to follow Satan's plan (he wanted to force us to do good), or Heavenly Father's plan (He wanted to give us the right to choose). We chose to follow Heavenly Father, so we were able to come to earth to receive a body. Because of this, we can choose for ourselves and progress to become like Heavenly Father and Jesus Christ.

Jesus promised that He would come to earth to die for us so that we can be resurrected and live again. He also promised that He would suffer for us so that we could be forgiven of our sins. Knowing this, we "shouted for joy" (Job 38:7). When we were born, we forgot about our life with Heavenly Father and Jesus.

Those who chose Satan's plan were cast down to earth, but they did not receive a body (Revelations 12:9). Satan and the spirits who followed him try to tempt us with their lies (Moses 4:4). Satan wants to get us to do wrong instead of right.

Because we chose to follow Jesus, we have moral agency. This means we can choose for ourselves good or bad. We love Jesus, so we want to do good, but sometimes we make a wrong choice and must repent. Each choice is followed by a reward or punishment. But we can choose for ourselves, and if we "do good," we will be rewarded (D&C 58:28).

Elder William R. Bradford of the Seventy explained that each of our actions, whether right or wrong, has a moral consequence. Christ's gospel shows us the difference between things that are right and good—which come from God—and things that are wrong and bad (see "Righteousness," *Ensign,* November 1999).

Christ has said: "And whatsoever thing persuadeth men to do good is of me; for good cometh of none save it be of me. I am the same that leadeth men to all good" (Ether 4:12).

*ACTIVITY

Play *Match Game* (right) to show what can happen when we make a good or bad choice. To make it easier to find a match, the pointed cards are choices and the indented cards are consequences. *To Play:* Mix cards and lay them facedown. Divide players into two teams. Each team takes turns turning cards over to make a

match. If a match is made, that team removes those two cards from the board. If no match is made, return the two cards facedown in same place. The team with the most matches wins.

CHALLENGE

Talk about the consequences for actions at home, school, and with friends, and how Heavenly Father blesses us when we make right choices. Brainstorm actions and consequences, good and bad.

TREATS

Choose the Right Crackers/Cookies. Give 4 graham crackers (or vanilla wafers or other small cookie or cracker) to each person. Each person can name a bad choice and crush the first cracker (as the bad choice). Brush the crumbs away and dispose (or put outside for birds). Next, eat three crackers and talk about three good choices.

MORE LESSON IDEAS: See *Primary Old Test. Manual 6,* lesson 2.

#15
BE STRONG AGAINST TEMPTATION

> **AHEAD OF TIME:** Print two sets of the *Temptation Traps Brainstorm and Match Game** (shown) using CD-ROM—codes: 15a and 15b (b&w), or 15aC and 15bC (color). To make, cut out cards (two sets of 12).

SONGS & SCRIPTURE

Sing "I'm Trying to Be like Jesus" and "Dare to Do Right" (*Children's Songbook,* 78, 158); read Ephesians 6:1.

SHORT LESSON

There are many "temptation traps" that keep us from choosing the right. If we fall into these traps by letting Satan tempt us, we give him power over us. Here are ways we can avoid temptation traps:

1. *Pray.* "Counsel with the Lord in all thy doings, and he will direct thee for good" (Alma 37:37). Prayer has power to protect us in this world of temptation. Prayer helps us face temptations and trials. As we pray each morning and night (and whenever we need to), we keep our focus on Heavenly Father's will and are less tempted to fall into Satan's traps.

2. *Be on the Lord's Side of the Fence.* If we are "in the middle" (undecided), we can be tempted. If we are "sitting on the fence" (undecided), it is hard to discern what is right and what is wrong. Satan can tempt those "in the middle" because they can be confused. We are always safe if we stay on the far side of the Lord's field and away from the "fence." If we stay on the Lord's side, it will be easier to resist temptation. If we are not sure if something is right, don't hesitate: avoid it. If in doubt, do without—say "no." When tempted, stop and look at the situation, then listen to the still small voice (the Holy Ghost) to avoid and resist Satan's traps (see Richard G. Scott, "Do What Is Right," *Ensign,* June 1997).

3. *Do As Jesus Would Do.* The more we learn about the life of our Savior Jesus Christ, His mission, and His example of righteousness, the easier it will be to follow Him, to do as He would do.

29

*ACTIVITY

Temptation Traps Brainstorm and Match Game.

• *Brainstorm.* Have family divide into two groups (going into separate rooms if desired). With a set of 12 *Temptation Trap* cards for each group, discuss the "escape route" you would take to avoid the temptation traps on each card and write answer on card. Then join the other group and combine all cards to play the match game.

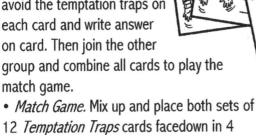

• *Match Game.* Mix up and place both sets of 12 *Temptation Traps* cards facedown in 4 rows of 6 cards on the floor or table. Each team takes turns lifting up the cards to make a match (returning cards facedown where you found them if no match is made). When a match is made, state the trap and discuss both escape routes as written on the cards. The team with the most matches wins.

CHALLENGE

Talk about the weight of sin and do some temptation weight lifting. Obtain some weights (or two cans of soup) and have a weight-lifting class. Discuss the weight Satan puts upon us if we accept his temptations. We have the power to push on through any temptation if we "hearken unto the word of God . . . the fiery darts of the adversary [will not] overpower [us] unto blindness, to lead [us] away to destruction" (1 Nephi 15:24).

TREATS

Box Cookies. Frost graham crackers together to create a box. Talk about how sin makes us feel boxed in, making it difficult to feel free. As we repent and avoid temptation traps, we exercise our right to the moral agency Jesus and Heavenly Father have given us. If we think ahead, we can avoid Satan's traps (1 Nephi 15:24).

MORE LESSON IDEAS: See *Young Women Manual 1,* lesson 28.

#16
HAPPY WHEN HONEST

SONGS & SCRIPTURE

Sing "I Pledge Myself to Love the Right" and "I Believe in Being Honest" (*Children's Songbook*, 16, 149); read Alma 27:27.

SHORT LESSON

When we are sincere, honest and truthful, others can trust us. In D&C 98:10, we learn that "Honest men and wise men should be sought for diligently."

The thirteenth Article of Faith emphasizes honesty: "We believe in being honest, true . . . . If there is anything virtuous, lovely, or of good report or praiseworthy, we seek after these things."

Other people may not know if you are honest or not, but you know, and so does your Heavenly Father. It makes you feel happy when you are honest. In Mosiah 2:41, King Benjamin asks us to "consider on the blessed and happy state of those that keep the commandments of God. For behold, they are blessed in all things, both temporal and spiritual."

President Gordon B. Hinckley explains that an honest boy or girl can have self-confidence, "standing above the crowd" of those who lie, cheat, and make excuses that lying hurts no one. Small lies lead to big lies, and we can see the proof in today's prisons (see "Great Shall Be the Peace of Thy Children," *Ensign,* November 2000).

*ACTIVITY

Talk about why we are happy when honest and unhappy when dishonest.
1. Show the two-sided *Puppet* (shown) by placing it over your hand or on the table in front of you and talking about decisions. When talking about honest decisions, flip to the smile side. For dishonest decisions, flip to the frown.
2. Take turns drawing and reading a wordstrip and flipping the *Puppet* to the happy or sad face to match the choice (honest or dishonest). You can compete in teams where the first to flip to the right face wins the point.

I am HAPPY when I am HONEST.

CHALLENGE

Talk about honest and dishonest decisions and what you will do if tempted to be dishonest. For example, you could tell of honest Abraham Lincoln. Before he became president of the United States, he was an "unsuccessful but successful" lawyer for 20 years. He was unsuccessful in terms of wealth but successful in terms of character, because he didn't like to charge people much who were as poor as he was. Once a man sent him $25, but Lincoln sent him back $10, saying he was being too generous.

TREATS

Honest-Face Pancakes. Color one-half cup of pancake batter blue and one-half cup red, using a drop or two of food coloring in each. Make oval-shaped pancakes. After turning the pancake, pour two drops of blue batter for the eyes and a streak of red batter for the smile. Then turn pancake over for 30 seconds to cook facial features. As children eat, think of honest decisions that make us happy.

MORE LESSON IDEAS: See *Primary Nursery Manual 1*, lesson 37.

#17

TELLING THE TRUTH

AHEAD OF TIME: *Print Trevor and Trina Truth Sack Puppets** (shown) using CD-ROM—codes: 17a and 17b (b&w), or 17aC and 17bC (color). To make puppets (for younger children), cut out puppets and glue the boy head on the *Trevor* sack and the girl head on the *Trina* sack. Then glue the body on the bottom with chin under flap.

SONGS & SCRIPTURE

Sing "My Dad" and "Our Primary Colors" (*Children's Songbook*, 211, 258); read 2 Nephi 2:6.

SHORT LESSON

We can be honest with Heavenly Father, others, and ourselves if we tell the truth. Proverbs 12:22 reads, "Lying lips are abomination to the LORD: but they that deal truly are his delight." Lying brings distrust. A person who is trustworthy is honest. If we are, our "confidence" will "wax strong in the presence of God" and our fellowman,
so "let virtue garnish thy thoughts unceasingly"(D&C 121:45).

      Follow Heavenly Father's and Jesus' example. They have promised to be truthful to us through the Holy Ghost. In Moroni 10:5–6 we learn, "And by the power of the Holy Ghost ye may know the truth of all things. And whatsoever thing is good is just and true." We in turn can be truthful to Heavenly Father and Jesus.

*ACTIVITY

Explain that thinking ahead will help you decide at a moment's notice what to do when you are tempted to be dishonest. With younger children, show the *Trevor Truth and Trina Truth Sack Puppets* to remind them that sometimes it's not easy to tell the truth, but with these puppets we can role-play truth-telling situations. When you move the sack flap up and down, the puppet's mouth opens to say "I can be strong and tell the truth."

33

Put on a puppet show, acting out different situations you might encounter with honesty. See if your audience agrees with your solutions to the situation. For older children, you don't need to use the puppets; just have them act out role-playing ideas themselves.

Role-play Ideas:

1. Trina goes up to Trevor and says, "Come on, let's ditch out on Samantha. I told her she could play, but I changed my mind."

2. Trevor tells Trina, "Look! Here are some free pretzels to try. Let's take a whole handful when they aren't looking."

CHALLENGE

Think of what your family would be like if members were dishonest with each other. Talk about the level of trust needed to make a happy family. For example, when you are away from home, your parents trust you to let them know where you are. President Thomas S. Monson encouraged us to be honest with our parents not only by avoiding lies, but also by simply communicating with them. If you can't avoid coming home late, you should call to let them know (see "Be Thou an Example," *Ensign,* May 2005).

TREATS

Tell the "Tooth" Gum. Purchase enough tooth-shaped white squares of gum for each person to have 4 to 5 pieces. (*Option:* If you have two dice, take turns throwing them until you get doubles to do the following.) Take turns explaining why it is important to tell the truth. Each time a person tells, pop another piece of gum in your mouth until you are chewing all 4 or 5 pieces. Then with your mouths full of gum, all of you say at once, "I will always tell the 'tooth.'"

More Lesson Ideas: See *Primary CTR-A Manual 2,* lesson 34.

#18
HONEST IN THOUGHT, WORD, & DEED

> **AHEAD OF TIME:** Print *Honesty Pays Game** (shown) using
> CD-ROM—codes: 18a and 18b (b&w), or 18aC and 18bC (color).
> To make, print 1 copy of game and 4 of *Blessing Buck* page; cut out.

SONGS & SCRIPTURE

Sing "Believe in Being Honest" and "Dare to Do Right" (*Children's Songbook,* 149, 158); read Alma 27:27.

SHORT LESSON

We make a promise when we agree to do something. When we are baptized, we make promises to Heavenly Father. One of these promises is to tell the truth, to keep our word.

When we are honest and keep our promises, others can trust us. We must think promises through very carefully before making them. Promises to Heavenly Father are the same way—we must think about our actions and make sure they are right.

*ACTIVITY

Help children learn the difference between good promises and bad promises. Even though children may be honest about keeping their promises, some promises are good and some are bad. Blessings come from keeping good promises.

Have children think about things they might promise to do (found on the game board, shown right). Discuss each promise and the consequences of making or breaking that promise.

Play the game (rules on pattern page). Tell children that the word "bucks" means money (in paper bills), which is a temporal reward, but *Blessing Bucks* are spiritual rewards that come from making and keeping good promises.

Honesty pays because we feel good about the promises we make, and because others trust us. You may want to bear your testimony of the value of being honest.

Bear your testimony of honesty. Testify that as people are honest, Heavenly Father will help and bless them.

CHALLENGE

Talk about blessings that come from honesty. Share blessing ideas, e.g., you are trusted with bigger and better things, you feel happy, you don't have to carry around guilt, Heavenly Father blesses you, it makes it easy for others to love you, you have peace of mind, it builds your character and strength so you can better serve others, you can have the guidance of the Holy Ghost.

TREATS

Honest- and Dishonest-Face Crackers. Using cheese from a can, squirt a smile on one cracker and a frown on the other. Talk about choices as you "chews" the right cookie as follows: As you chew on the frowny face cookie, talk about wrong choices. As you chew on the smiley face cookie, talk about right choices that bring you peace and happiness.

MORE LESSON IDEAS: See *Primary Old Testament Manual 6*, lesson 14.

#19

HONEST TITHES

> ***AHEAD OF TIME:*** Print 2 sets of the *Tithing Helps Match Game**
> (shown) using CD-ROM—codes: 19 (b&w) or 19C (color) on card
> stock. To make, cut out cards.

SONGS & SCRIPTURE

Sing "I Want to Give the Lord My Tenth" and "I'm Glad to Pay a Tithing"
(*Children's Songbook,* 150); read Malachi 3:10–11.

SHORT LESSON

Heavenly Father has given us the law of tithing, asking us to pay one-tenth
of our earnings to the Church to build up the kingdom of God on the earth.
The money is used for temples and churches, for missionary work, to
support redemption of the dead, and for other purposes our Church leaders
deem necessary (see Dallin H. Oaks, "Tithing," *Ensign,* May 1994). If we
pay an honest tithe we not only serve, we help pay Heavenly Father back for
blessings received (3 Nephi 24:8).

When we pay our tithing, we receive blessings as stated in Malachi
3:10–11: (1) the Lord will open "the windows of heaven" and "pour out
blessings, that there shall not be room enough to receive it"; (2) the Lord
will "rebuke the devourer . . . and he shall not destroy the fruits of your
ground." This means that we will have enough to eat.

Elder Dallin H. Oaks said that his mother, a widow, paid her tithing
even on a schoolteacher's small income. She told him that they could not
get along without paying tithing. She explained that she could not raise her
children as a single parent without the blessings of the Lord she received by
paying an honest tithe. The Lord has promised to bless us when we pay our
tithing (see "Tithing," *Ensign,* May 1994).

* ACTIVITY

Play the *Tithing Helps Match Game* to learn that: (1) Tithing helps build temples and meetinghouses, (2) Tithing helps support missionary work, (3) Tithing helps support family history and temple work, (4) Heavenly Father will bless us when we pay our tithing, and (5) I am happy to help by paying my tithing. *To Play:* Mix up cards and turn them facedown. Take turns turning two cards over for others to see. If a match is made, player collects the two matching cards. Player reads the card aloud to others, i.e., "Tithing helps missionary work." Play until all cards are matched and read aloud.

CHALLENGE

Talk about paying our tithing first before spending our money, reading about the widow's mite (Mark 12:43–44).

TREATS

Tithing Toast. Read D&C 64:23–24; D&C 85:3. Say, "We can become 'toast' in the latter days when the earth is cleansed by fire if we do not pay our tithing." To make toast, butter bread and sprinkle with sugar. Broil to melt (2 to 3 minutes). *Optional:* Use yellow or green sugar, then cut toast into round coins or rectangular dollar bills.

MORE LESSON IDEAS: See *Primary CTR-B Manual 3,* lesson 42.

#20

REVERENCE THE NAMES OF GOD
THE FATHER AND THE SON

AHEAD OF TIME: Print *Reverent Mouth Pop-Up** using CD-ROM—codes: 20 (b&w) or 20C1 and 20C2 (color). To make, cut out face and mouth piece. Cut a slit in the mouth where indicated. Insert mouth piece through slit. Fold and glue down mouth piece tab on the back side of the face.

SONGS & SCRIPTURE

Sing "Reverence Is Love" and "The Church of Jesus Christ" (*Children's Songbook*, 31, 77); read Mosiah 13:15.

SHORT LESSON

It is important to Heavenly Father and Jesus Christ that we use Their names reverently and not in vain. This means we should not use the names of Heavenly Father and Jesus Christ when we are not really thinking of Them. We also should keep our speech clean by not swearing or using crude words.

Elder Dallin H. Oaks tells us that when we use God's or Jesus' names in vain or without authority, it is profanity (swearing). It is wrong for us to use Their names in a hateful or angry way, or as an exclamation in our everyday speech. We can use the names of the Father and the Son with authority when we teach of Them with reverence, when we pray respectfully, and during administration of priesthood ordinances (see "Reverent and Clean," *Ensign,* May 1986).

We can use the name of Christ reverently as we talk of Him, His mission in life, His teachings, His sacrifice, and His love. We can read about those who testify of Him in the scriptures. His Church is called by His name—The Church of Jesus Christ of Latter-day Saints. But whenever we speak His name it should be done in reverence.

*ACTIVITY

Flap the *Reverent Mouth Pop-Up* up and down and memorize the verse. Look up the scripture references to find and fill in the missing words below the *Pop-Up,* then glue the statements on the back.

The first scripture reference, 2 Nephi 26:32, explains that the consequence of disobeying this commandment (and others) is serious: "They should not

take the name of the Lord their God in vain . . . they should do none of these things; for whoso doeth them shall perish." What does *perish* mean? It refers to death, but in a spiritual way. The world does not understand this, but we as members of His church—The Church of Jesus Christ of Latter-day Saints—can be good examples by using God's and Jesus' names only in reverent ways.

CHALLENGE

Think of ways to show honor to Heavenly Father and Jesus by treating Their names reverently (e.g., pray with a sincere heart; ponder covenants during sacrament and commit to always remember Him; do not make jokes using Their names; etc.).

TREATS

Lip-shaped Gelatin Blocks or Lip-shaped Gummy Candy. Lip-shaped treats will remind us to speak with respect. To create the gelatin blocks stir 2 large (6 oz.) packages of flavored gelatin (such as Jell-O) and approximately 2 1/2 cups boiling water for 3 minutes. Pour into a 9" x 13" pan and chill for 3 hours. Set bottom of pan in warm water, then release gelatin onto a cutting board. Cut out mouth shapes with cookie cutter or knife.

MORE LESSON IDEAS: See *Primary CTR-B Manual 3,* lesson 43.

#21

SHOW RESPECT

> *AHEAD OF TIME:* Print *Respectful Choices Poster** (shown) using CD-ROM—codes: 21a and 21b (b&w), or 21aC and 21bC (color).

SONGS & SCRIPTURE

Sing "I Thank Thee Dear Father" and "To Think about Jesus" (*Children's Songbook,* 7, 71); read D&C 38:24.

SHORT LESSON

Jesus taught us to love God and to love one another. A way we can show our love is by being respectful. To respect someone means to consider them of worth or value. We can show we respect for others by how we talk to and treat them. Following are some ways we can show respect to Heavenly Father and Jesus:

- *Pray Appropriately*—to show that we look up to Heavenly Father and Jesus. Ordinance prayers such as the sacrament always use the same words, but personal prayers should come from the heart. Try to use suitable words for the language of prayer: "Thee" and "Thou" (instead of "you"), "Thy" (instead of "your"), and "Thine" (instead of "yours").
- *Dress Modestly*—to show we respect our body, which is a "temple of the Holy Ghost" (1 Corinthians 6:19). Be modest in dress by not being led astray by the world's fashion standards, which sometimes are immodest.
- *Be Kind to Others*—All of Heavenly Father's children are important to Him. We can show we respect God's children by giving of our time, a listening ear, or an understanding heart.
- *Use Good Words*—Express praise by saying things like "Good job!" or "That's a great idea!" Avoid mean or rude words. In Colossians 3:8, we are told to "put off . . . filthy communication out of your mouth." Using dirty words pollutes the mind and heart of both the speaker and the

listener. Heavenly Father wants us to be clean so we can live with Him again someday.

- *Listen Politely*—Let others speak without interrupting them. Pay attention to what they are saying. Once they are finished, you can speak.
- *Say "Please" and "Thank You"*—Saying "please" shows we respect another person's agency. Saying "thank you" shines a light on the other person for their good deeds.

*ACTIVITY

Show the *Respectful Choices Poster* and talk about making respectful choices ahead of time. Cut out, match, and glue on the pictures with the RESPECT and DISRESPECT categories on the chart.

CHALLENGE

Talk about ways your family members can show respect toward each other, others, and Heavenly Father.

Write the word *RESPECT* on a page in a left column. Then use those letters to write words of respectful actions. For example (ways to show respect for Heavenly Father): "R" Remember the Sabbath day to keep it holy, "E" Be an example, "S" Partake of the sacrament reverently, "P" Follow the prophet, "E" Enter Heavenly Father's house with reverence, "C" Choose the right, "T" Bear testimony that the gospel is true.

TREATS

CTR Cookies. Frost the letters *CTR* on a cookie to remind children that as they choose the right each day, they are showing respect and love for Heavenly Father and Jesus.

MORE LESSON IDEAS: See *Primary New Test. Manual 7,* lesson 8.

#22

RIGHTEOUS SABBATH ACTIVITIES

> *AHEAD OF TIME:* Print the *Sabbath-Day Activity Box** label, glue-on stickers (shown), and *Super Sunday Sabbath Day Activities List* using CD-ROM—codes: 22a, 22b, and 22c (b&w); or 22aC, 22bC, and 22cC (color). To make a *Sabbath Day Activity Box*, find a large box with a lid and cover it with wrapping paper or paint. Cut out the *Sabbath-Day Activity Box* label and suns; glue these on box lid and box. Then add the *Super Sunday Sabbath Day Activities List*.

SONGS & SCRIPTURE

Sing "Remember the Sabbath Day" and "When I Go to Church" (*Children's Songbook*, 155, 157); read Mosiah 18:23.

SHORT LESSON

Choosing to keep the Sabbath day holy will bring great blessings to you and your family. The Sabbath is a day of rest and worship. It is important that we choose the right Sunday activities.

We can easily sacrifice great blessings if we choose to participate in certain activities that don't invite the spirit of worship. Examples of these could include going shopping, fishing, hunting, golfing, amusement seeking, joy riding, or to sporting events or movies.

The Sabbath is a day to:

1. Learn about the gospel and teachings of Jesus, to learn how to follow Him and apply correct principles.
2. Study the scriptures and to think about life's eternal purposes.
3. Feast upon spiritual things.
4. Rest from worldly work.
5. Enjoy family, righteous activities, and friendship.

*ACTIVITY

Make and fill the *Sabbath-Day Activity Box* with Sabbath-worthy ideas and supplies. Talk about how you feel the Spirit when you are engaged in worthy Sabbath-day activities. Read Exodus 20:8–11.

CHALLENGE

Plan ahead so you and your family can enjoy worthy Sabbath-day activities before and after church. Talk about the importance of sharing the Sabbath day with your family. Write select activities on cards so you can try one or two each week. Keep adding Sabbath-worthy games and activities to the box, along with items needed to make Sunday a day to look forward to.

Create Sabbath-Day Activity Cards. On cards, write categories of good things to do on the Sabbath, then add ideas to the cards under that category. Examples: Meal Time, Music and Singing, Rest Time, Scripture Reading, Church Magazine Reading, Family Home Evening (if you don't have it on Monday), Spiritual Games, Articles of Faith and Scripture Memorization, Washing Dishes (include ideas to make it more restful), Talking Time, Letter Writing, Scrapbook and Journal Time, Goal-setting Time, Interviews with Parents, Problem-solving Time, Visiting Needy, etc.

TREATS

"Sun"day Cake. Frost a 2-layer cake with bright yellow frosting (heavy on sides). Stick wafer cookies on side to make sun rays. Talk about how righteous Sabbath-day activities will help you create a sunny disposition and spread sunshine on "Sun"day with your family.

CHOOSE SABBATH ACTIVITIES THAT WILL HELP
ME FEEL CLOSE TO HEAVENLY FATHER & JESUS CHRIST

#23

SWEET SABBATH DAY

AHEAD OF TIME: Print *Sabbath Day Activity Advent Calendar** (shown) using CD-ROM—codes: 23 (b&w) or 23C (color). To make, cut out and cut between each wordstrip, so that when activity is completed it can be folded and torn off. Punch holes at the top of calendar and tie a 20" piece of yarn to hang it on the wall. *Candy Treat:* Ahead of time, place 14 pieces of candy in a zip- or snap-close plastic bag.

SONGS & SCRIPTURE

Sing "The Commandments" and "Saturday" (*Children's Songbook,* 112, 196); read Exodus 20:10–11.

SHORT LESSON

The Sabbath is a special day when we can do things that help us feel close to Heavenly Father and Jesus. We are asked to keep it holy: "Remember the sabbath day, to keep it holy" (Mosiah 13:6). The Sabbath day can be "sweet" if you make it a day of worship and family time. Keeping it holy helps us feel the Spirit and receive blessings.

Each week on days one through six, we can prepare so that on day seven we can worship. Look ahead to decide what you will do on the Sabbath and what preparations are necessary. What are some things we can do to get ready for Sunday?

1. Write talks and prepare church lessons ahead of time. If we are having family home evening on Sunday, prepare lessons and treats in advance.
2. Do house and yard work; get the work done before playing on Saturday.
3. Have your Saturday-night bath and get your Sunday clothes ready.
4. Make sure you get plenty of exercise and rest on Saturday.
5. Make sure your attitude is ready for learning and worship.

*ACTIVITY

For the next 14 weeks, challenge your family to try one of these 14 activities each Sunday to keep this special day holy. Read instructions on the calendar: "Try an activity and tear off the wordstrip below. Then enjoy a treat in a bag and say, 'It's sweet to honor the Sabbath day!'" Give each family member a bag of candy treats to keep by calendar. When they complete one of the activities they can remove it from calendar and receive a treat.

SABBATH DAY ACTIVITY·ADVENT·CALENDAR

14 DAYS 14 WAYS — TO KEEP THE SABBATH DAY HOLY!

Try an activity and tear off the wordstrip below. Then enjoy a treat in the bag and say, "It's sweet to honor the Sabbath day."

14. Make a family of appreciation for family members.
13. Take turns acting out and guessing scripture stories.
12. Visit someone who is ill or lonely.
11. Look at family photographs.
10. Read your holy journal or family history.
9. Play quiet game with your brother or sister.
8. Give a family home evening lesson.
7. Visit relatives.
6. Study the scriptures.
5. Listen to sacred music.
4. Write in your journal.
3. Read a scripture day to a brother or sister.
2. Visit an older member in the ward.
1. Write a letter to a missionary.

CHALLENGE

Talk about the blessings that can come from each of the Sabbath day activities on the calendar. Each Sunday ask family to share their feelings about these special activities. *Examples (found on the Advent Calendar) and Blessings:* (1) *Example:* "Writing a special letter to a missionary" that he/she can treasure. Fill it with gospel quotes to inspire and scriptures that have touched your heart. *Blessing:* Your testimony will grow. (2) *Example:* "Visiting an older member of the ward." Go out of your comfort zone and think of ways you can cheer and bless and brighten. *Blessing:* You learn wisdom, patience, love, and understanding from them.

TREATS

Manna (Bread). Purchase or bake round loaves of bread on Saturday to serve on Sunday. The Israelites were told not to gather manna on Sunday, but on the sixth day they could gather enough for the Sabbath. (Read Exodus 16:19–20.) What happened when they disobeyed and gathered manna on the Sabbath? (See Exodus 16:22–25.) How can we apply this principle to our weekly preparation for the Sabbath?

MORE LESSON IDEAS: See *Primary Old Testament Manual 6,* lesson 20.

#24
SEARCH & PONDER SCRIPTURES

AHEAD OF TIME: Print *Search & Ponder Bookmark** (shown) using CD-ROM—codes: heart border 24a or 24b (b&w), or sun border 24aC or 24bC (color). Cut out bookmark; laminate if desired. Obtain a notebook, pencil, and a colored scripture-underlining pencil.

SONGS & SCRIPTURE
Sing "Seek the Lord Early" and "Search, Ponder, and Pray" (*Children's Songbook,* 108, 109); read 2 Nephi 4:15.

SHORT LESSON
One of the best things to do on the Sabbath (and every day) is to read the scriptures. "Behold, the scriptures are before you" (Alma 13:20). We are blessed to have the scriptures in our day. They were written long ago, but many were actually written for us in our day.

Elder David A. Bednar, an Apostle, teaches that we should study the Book of Mormon so we can prepare to have the constant companionship of the Holy Ghost (see "That We May Always Have His Spirit to Be with Us," *Ensign,* May 2006).

In Moroni 10:4–5 we are promised that if we pray we can receive a testimony of the Book of Mormon, "And when ye shall receive these things, I would exhort you that ye would ask God, the Eternal Father, in the name of Christ, if these things are not true; and if ye shall ask with a sincere heart, with real intent, having faith in Christ, he will manifest the truth of it unto you, by the power of the Holy Ghost. And by the power of the Holy Ghost ye may know the truth of all things."

If we read the scriptures and ponder them in our heart, our soul will "delight in the scriptures" (2 Nephi 4:15) and our testimony will grow.

ACTIVITY

For older children: Find a subject you are interested in as a family and search scriptures on that subject using the Topical Guide references. Read scripture footnotes that cross-reference other scriptures, then turn to those. You could have a scripture chase where you compete to find the scriptures mentioned. For younger children: Have each child choose a favorite scripture story to have parents read/tell (use a scripture picture book if desired, e.g., Book of Mormon Stories by the Church).

*CHALLENGE

Have family members read the *Search and Ponder Bookmark.* Challenge them to keep the bookmark in their scriptures and follow the steps. They can use the edge to underline key scriptures with colored pencils. Discuss the five steps:

Step 1: Start with prayer. Pray to understand what you read, and for answers to any specific questions/ problems you have.

Step 2: Have paper and pencil ready. Inspiration often comes as we read the scriptures, so we should have a place to write it down.

Steps 3–5: Take your time reading and ask questions. If you care more about *what* you are reading than *how much* you are reading, you will learn more. Stop to ponder; think about the meaning as you read the verse again. Then pray for understanding, asking questions in your mind and waiting for impressions. Then write them down.

TREATS

Heart-shaped Cookies. Tell family that each time we read the scriptures, our hearts and minds can feel the Holy Ghost bear witness of the scriptures' truthfulness. Have family share truths that they have experienced while searching and pondering the scriptures.

#25
STRENGTHEN FAMILY

AHEAD OF TIME: Print *Family Life Can Be a Picnic Tent Card* * (shown) using CD-ROM—codes: 25 (b&w), or 25C1 or 25C2 (color). To make, cut around outer border of *Tent Card,* then dotted lines around family. Fold over card at halfway mark, allowing illustration to stand up on top.

SONGS & SCRIPTURE

Sing "Family Night" and "And Quickly I'll Obey" (*Children's Songbook,* 195, 196); read Alma 37:35.

SHORT LESSON

We can honor our parents and strengthen our family by having a good attitude and obeying the Lord's commandments.

In the Book of Mormon, the prophet Lehi chose to follow the Lord when he was instructed to "take his family and depart into the wilderness" (1 Nephi 2:2). It was hard to travel and live in the desert, and two of Lehi's sons, Laman and Lemuel, complained and were disrespectful to their parents. Lehi led his family to a land of promise, but it was not a place of peace, because Laman and Lemuel continued to disobey the Lord. This brought sorrow to Lehi's heart (2 Nephi 1:17). Before he died, Lehi gathered his children to bless and counsel them (2 Nephi 1:21; 4:5), urging Laman and Lemuel to repent and be faithful (2 Nephi 1:23).

Father Lehi taught all his children the principles of the gospel, but Laman and Lemuel did not listen. If they had listened and obeyed, they would have been happy, but they did not, so they made the journey to the promised land difficult for their whole family. What might they have done differently to strengthen their family?

What are we doing to love and strengthen our families? As we care for each other, our family is strengthened. "Thee lift me and I'll lift thee, and we'll ascend together" (Quaker proverb).

*ACTIVITY

Talk about how a happy attitude and going the extra mile to love and support your family makes your family strong. Part of honoring your parents is to honor each family member. Read the *Tent Card:* "Life with family can be a picnic if I understand my role as a family member." Write three ways you c-"an't" go wrong

Life with my family can be a picnic if I understand my role as a family member.

I will be a particip"ant" and show love and support by doing the following:

🐜 _____

🐜 _____

🐜 _____

by being a particip"ant" in showing love and support to your family.

Ideas: Start each day with a smile or a song; make your bed; pray for family; rise early to get ready so you will have time to help; listen; praise; clean up messes; get homework done without nagging; help younger brothers and sisters with homework, chores, and problems; help prepare family home evening; fix meals; do the dishes; remind family of family prayer; save your money to help with emergencies and gifts; call and visit grandparents or relatives; remember birthdays and special days.

CHALLENGE

Brainstorm more ways family members can make family life a "picnic" (to place on *Tent Card*, shown above).

TREATS

Option #1—Family Picnic. Enjoy a picnic together indoors or outdoors. If it's summer, include watermelon and corn, but don't forget the sandwiches and cake (like on the *Tent Card*, shown above)!

Option #2—Popcorn. As you wait for popcorn to pop, sing "The Family" (*Children's Songbook,* 41) for a closing song. (One verse talks about "popping popcorn and having fun.")

#26

COMMUNICATE WITH FAMILY

AHEAD OF TIME: Print *Soar High Cross-Match Puzzle** (shown) using CD-ROM—codes: 26 (b&w) or 26C (color).

SONGS & SCRIPTURE

Sing "The Family" and "Here We Are Together" (*Children's Songbook,* 194, 261); read Proverbs 15:1–2.

SHORT LESSON

We can strengthen our family by improving family communication. Here are five things we can do to communicate well:

1. *Help Create a Good Environment for Communication.* Elder L. Tom Perry observed that quality family life has been replaced by microwaved dinners in front of the TV. Instead, we should be interacting as we eat, study, play, and work together (see "Therefore I Was Taught," *Ensign,* May 1994). Talk about activities that will give family members more opportunities to communicate.

2. *Accept Members of the Family As They Are, and Give Compliments of Approval.* Elder Marlin K. Jensen suggested that our desire for friendship and acceptance can be largely satisfied within the home. It's wonderful if children consider their parents to be some of their best friends (see "Friendship: A Gospel Principle," *Ensign,* May 1999). In order to be friends, we need to criticize each other less and praise each other more. Talk about ways family members can be friends.

3. *Be Affectionate.* "Never put off until tomorrow what you can do today" is good advice when it comes to expressing affection. Love missed today will make tomorrow gloomy. Love expressed today will make tomorrow memorable and warm. Talk about ways family members can show affection. Share things your family has done that help you to feel loved.

4. *Confide in Parents and Other Family Members, and Keep the Confidences Shared with You.* A teen suggested, "Confide in your parents. This means that you keep them informed about your basic feelings, fears, and

aspirations. As you confide in them you usually strengthen your goals and interests and overcome fears and problems. In turn, you strengthen the family." Discuss why it's important to keep confidences that are shared with you.

5. *Care about Interests of Family Members and Be a Good Listener.* If we put our interests aside and think about the needs of our family, we will grow closer, blessing one another. Elder Robert D. Hales explained that we miss the chance to truly listen and understand each other when we are thinking about our own selfish wants. We need to consider each other's feelings and needs (see "How Will Our Children Remember Us?" *Ensign,* Nov. 1993).

*ACTIVITY

Do the *Soar High Cross-Match Puzzle* to learn eight ways to see how much you know about communication.

CHALLENGE

Have each family member choose one way they wish to communicate better (see *"TREATS"* below) and work on it, reporting their experiences the next week or month.

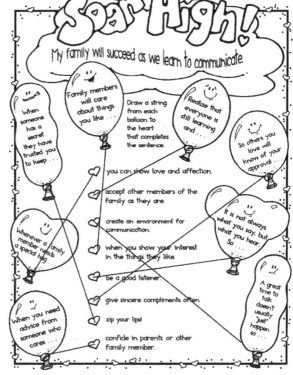

TREATS

Soaring High Pudding Painting. Make several different colors of pudding (e.g., chocolate, pistachio, butterscotch, and vanilla) and paint balloons on waxed paper. Then eat the balloons with fingers as each person explains how he or she has chosen to *Soar High* to improve family communication.

MORE LESSON IDEAS: See *Young Women Manual 2,* lesson 8.

#27
GET TO KNOW EXTENDED FAMILY

AHEAD OF TIME: Print *Closeness Checklist and Postcard** (shown) using CD-ROM—codes: 27 (b&w) or 27C (color). Color and cut out.

SONGS & SCRIPTURE

Sing "I Have a Family Tree" and "Grandmother" (*Children's Songbook,* 199, 200); read Malachi 4:6.

SHORT LESSON

Let's make time to include our extended family in our circle of love, remembering that families are forever. If we begin now to develop strong family ties, we will not be alone when we are separated from our immediate family. We will have someone we can call or communicate with when we're in need, and someone we can serve.

Here are some fun ideas to get close to your extended family:

• *Have a Grammy Awards Night.* Create a potluck dinner for your grandmother or grandfather. Spotlight the grandparent, then award him or her with a Grammy Award certificate and a giant cookie.

• *Have a "Relative"-ly Fun Night.* Create a fun night to include one of your favorite relatives you live near. Relatives can share how they remember the family member, spotlighting each other. Play fun games to get acquainted. Play games relatives played as a kid (e.g., "kick the can," Pac-Man, etc.)

• *Send Greeting Cards.* Compile a list of family birthdays and send cards.

• *Get Acquainted with Extended Family through Photos.* Gather photos of extended family members. Tell about each person, expressing why you love him or her. Share an experience or story about each person. Explain that when we spend time with our extended family, we create lasting memories we can share with our children one day using photos and our journal.

53

ACTIVITY

Follow these steps to become close to your extended family:

1. Use the *Family Closeness Checklist* to plan what you will do to get closer to a member of your extended family.
2. Circle or highlight several things you wish to do in the following year to become close to that person. Schedule these actions on a calendar this week.

3. Begin by sending the extended family member a *Postcard* (shown). Decorate the front, write a quick note, and send it off this week!

CHALLENGE

Invent activities where you can get close to extended family members. *Ideas:* Include them in vacation plans, invite them to your home, organize a family reunion. (See *Closeness Checklist* ideas.)

TREATS

Close Encounters of the Marshmallow Kind S'mores. The 1977 movie *Close Encounters of the Third Kind* is about aliens from outer space. Even when your relatives are in "outer space" (far away), you can still have "close encounters" with them. To make *S'mores*, microwave a marshmallow until it melts (a few seconds). Then place it between graham crackers with chocolate squares, waiting for the chocolate to melt before eating. Discuss ways to have "close encounters" with relatives that live far away. Then schedule time with them, to have an out-of-this-world experience.

MORE LESSON IDEAS: See *Young Women Manual 3*, lesson 11.

#28
HARMONY AT HOME

> ***AHEAD OF TIME:*** Print *Love at Home Spin-the-Bottle** label and wordstrips (shown) using CD-ROM—codes: 28a and 28b (b&w), or 28aC and 28bC (color). To make, mount label on a jar and place wordstrips inside, adding more that fit your family.

SONGS & SCRIPTURE

Sing "Love Is Spoken Here" and "When We're Helping" (*Children's Songbook*, 190, 198); read Mosiah 4:14–15.

SHORT LESSON

Home is a place where we can feel harmony and peace when love is nurtured, truth is learned, and integrity is cultivated.

To achieve family harmony, our highest priorities should be family prayer, family home evening, family gospel study and instruction, and wholesome family activities.

1. *Family Prayer.* "Pray in your families unto the Father, always in my name, that your wives and your children may be blessed" (3 Nephi 18:21). We are encouraged to have family prayer twice a day. President Spencer W. Kimball explained that family prayer once a day might have been all right in the past, but that now "it will not be enough if we are going to save our families" (*Finding Light in a Dark World*, 91). (See also Gordon B. Hinckley, "The Blessings of Family Prayer, *Ensign,* Feb. 1991.)

2. *Family Home Evening.* Great blessings come from obeying the prophets' counsel to have family home evening each week. President Joseph F. Smith said these blessings include an increase of love among family members, and the ability to make good choices when faced with temptation (see James R. Clark, comp., *Messages of the First Presidency of The Church of Jesus Christ of Latter-day Saints,* 4:339).

3. *Gospel Study and Instruction.* Reading the scriptures as a family—as well as the everyday lessons parents teach—can help family members stay close to the Lord and develop wisdom.

4. *Wholesome Family Activities.* Working and playing together strengthens our relationships and makes great memories. Elder Gene R. Cook stated that family activities enrich our family life with "fun, zest, and spark." He also said that for maximum success, children should be involved in planning the activities. (See *Raising Up a Family to the Lord,* 299).

*ACTIVITY

Have family tell how they would show love in each situation by playing *Love at Home Spin-the-Bottle* (shown). Rules are on bottle label.

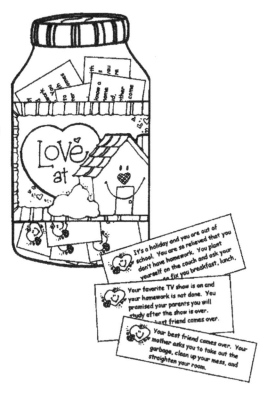

CHALLENGE

Plan when you will have family prayer, family home evening, family scripture and gospel study, and your next family activity.

TREATS

Family Ties Necklace. Thread a strand of string licorice through ten or more pretzels to form a necklace. Tie the licorice to each pretzel to keep them apart. *Thought:* As we make the right choices each day, we create family ties. Deciding to be cheerful, kind, neat, helpful, and thoughtful increases love and harmony, keeping the family close.

MORE LESSON IDEAS: See *Young Women Manual 2,* lesson 7.

#29
SHARING WORK

> **AHEAD OF TIME:** Print *Home "Tweet" Home No-Mess Nest Routine**
> (shown) using CD-ROM—codes: 29 (b&w) or 29C (color). To make, cut
> out parts A and B. Attach bird arrow on wheel with a paper fastener.

SONGS & SCRIPTURE

Sing "When We're Helping" and "The Prophet Said to Plant a Garden"
(*Children's Songbook,* 198, 247); read D&C 88:119.

SHORT LESSON

Most children are assigned chores in the home and/or yard. In homes where
parents attend college or have more than one job, children often have to do
many chores to help out.

Sharing work strengthens a family. At the beginning of each week,
sit down as a family and list important tasks, dividing the work so that
everyone takes part in making the house a home. Learning to work will not
only develop character—it will prepare us for greater opportunities. When
family members cheerfully accept extra duties, they lighten the load for
others and bring peace and happiness into the home.

Talk about the following rooms in the home and ask, "Are they
neat?" (Modify these as needed to best describe your home.)

1. *The Kitchen, the Hub of the Home:* A place to prepare meals, eat
   together, discuss the day's events, prepare treats for family home
   evening, and cook dinner for a needy neighbor.
2. *The Living Room, the Conversation Pit:* A place for family home evening,
   family prayer, family scripture study, and family council. A place where
   the home teachers visit to share a gospel lesson.

Now take the same approach with the outdoor areas around your
home. Are there any outdoor chores that need to be discussed?

ACTIVITY

Taking care of daily chores will help make home a more pleasant place. Write daily tasks on the *Home "Tweet" Home No-Mess Nest Routine*. Challenge your family to make a habit of doing these chores each day. *Ideas:* put away toys, sweep floors, do a load of laundry, iron, do dishes, organize desk, hang clothes in closet.

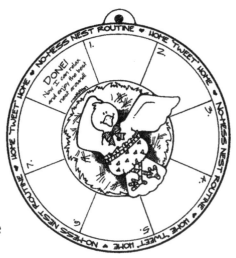

CHALLENGE

Encourage help at home using the following:

1. *Job Jar and Job General.* Help family create their own "job jar" label to place on a jar, as well as job wordstrips to place inside jar. Have family work with a "job general," who is in charge for the week. Have each person draw a job from the jar, tell the general the job, and report back to him or her when the job is complete.

2. *Timer Tactics.* Divide family into teams of two and have them go through the house, garage, or yard with a timer in hand. Give teams five to ten minutes per room or area. Ask them to beat the clock and clean, organize, or weed the area before the timer rings. With two people working together, work is enjoyable, and two can get twice as much done as one.

3. *Closet or Cupboard Concentration.* Offer ideas on how to keep a closet clean. Have two family members work together on one closet/cupboard. *Ideas:* Hang clothes grouped by items or color, keep empty hangers in front, put dirty clothes in hamper.

TREATS

Graham-cracker Birdhouse. Form an edible birdhouse by frosting graham crackers together and topping with candies. Talk about ways to make home a "tweet" (sweet) place to live.

MORE LESSON IDEAS: See *Young Women Manual 2*, lesson 6.

#30
PURE THOUGHTS

AHEAD OF TIME: Print *Mind Power Wheel* *(shown) using CD-ROM—codes: 30a and 30b (b&w), or 30aC1 or 30aC2 and 30bC (color). To make, cut hair off around face for boys and leave hair on for girls. Cut window out at the top of head. Attach wheel on back of head by placing a paper fastener or "button brad" through the center dots. (To make button brad, sew two buttons together on opposite sides—threading thread through the same holes—to attach head to wheel.

SONGS & SCRIPTURE

Sing "Hum Your FavoriteHymn" and "The Lord Gave Me a Temple" (*Children's Songbook*, 152, 153); read JST Proverbs 15:26 or 1 Corinthians 3:16–17.

SHORT LESSON

President David O. Mckay taught that "the strength of this Church lies in the purity of the thoughts and lives of its members" (*Conference Report*, Oct. 1967). In JST Proverbs 15:26, we read, "The thoughts of the wicked are an abomination to the Lord; but the words of the pure are pleasant words."

Having pure thoughts all the time is a challenge, but it can be done if every day we clean the house inside our head.

A head filled with bad thoughts is like a house filled with garbage—it must be cleaned out before anything good can enter. If our head is empty— if we're not busy thinking of good things—bad thoughts can enter. (Read Matthew 12:43-45—the parable of the empty house.) *More Ideas:* See Boyd K. Packer, *That All May Be Edified* (Salt Lake City: Bookcraft, 1982), 196.

What can we do to fill our mind with good thoughts? We can get rid of books, movies, games, and other media that feed our mind with bad thoughts, then replace them with good books, good movies, good games, and good friends with similar values.

We can search the scriptures and learn Primary songs and hymns to occupy our mind when impure or unclean thoughts arise. We can keep bad thoughts out by replacing them with a verse or a melody. We can stay tuned in to righteous thoughts.

Learning the gospel will also strengthen our desire to be pure in mind and heart. Our testimony of Jesus Christ will help each of us withstand evil. The word *EVIL* spelled backwards is *LIVE*. Evil brings death to the spirit, but inviting pure thoughts and living as Jesus would live brings life and happiness.

* ACTIVITY

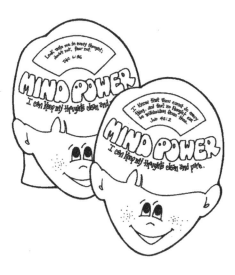

Create *Mind Power Wheel* (shown) to remind us to develop "wheelie" good thoughts. Take turns turning the wheel to read the scriptures that tell us how to keep our thoughts clean and pure.

CHALLENGE

Talk about how choosing right begins with choosing clean and pure thoughts. What we think in our mind becomes what we desire in our heart, and what swells within our heart becomes our actions.

SWEET TREATS

Sweet and Sour "Thought" Treats. Talk about how frosted cupcakes are sweet like the gospel of Jesus Christ, and how dill pickles are sour like the way we feel when our thoughts and actions are not pure. As we learn about the gospel and choose the right, our thoughts grow sweeter. *Option:* Frost *CTR* on cupcakes.

MORE LESSON IDEAS: See *Primary Old Testament Manual 6*, lesson 30.

#31

TUNE INTO RIGHTEOUS THOUGHTS

> ***AHEAD OF TIME:*** Print *Righteous Radio** (shown) using CD-ROM—
> codes: 31 (b&w) or 31C (color). To make, cut line above the word
> "Righteous" with razor blade. Fold arrow as shown. Fit arrow into slit,
> then slide arrow dial back & forth. *Option:* Glue buttons on as knobs.

SONGS & SCRIPTURE

Sing "Dare to Do Right" and "Tell Me, Dear Lord" (*Children's Songbook,*
159, 176); read Mosiah 4:30.

SHORT LESSON

To keep our mind and body pure, we can tune in to the good "stations" on
the *Righteous Radio* (shown). We can pray, study and meditate on the
Lord's plan and the scriptures, follow the Holy Ghost, choose good friends,
and treasure the prophet's words and our patriarchal blessing. When we're
righteous, we can tune in to the Lord's will.

Talk about the media influences in our lives—radio, television,
satellite, cable, movies, video games, the internet, etc.—and what to look
for (the good) and what to avoid (the bad). *Ideas:*

1. *Good:* Talk about the good things that good media brings to our lives,
   e.g., beautiful music, educational programs, family history research.
2. *Bad:* Talk about the bad things that bad media brings to our lives, the
   mixed signals (good and bad presented together), and Satan's design
   for the use of media, e.g., pornography, music with dirty lyrics, gossip.

For additional information, see the following: Spencer J. Condie,
"Mushrooms, Music, Movies, and Magazines," *New Era,* Feb. 1990; David E.
Sorensen, "You Can't Pet a Rattlesnake, *Ensign,* May 2001; Joseph Walker,
"Reel Life vs. Real Life," *Ensign,* June 1993. (See also lds.org—click on
"Gospel Topics" and search for the word "media.")

*ACTIVITY

Using the *Righteous Radio* (shown), review five ways we can stay tuned in to righteous thoughts through prayer, study and meditation, Holy Ghost, good friends, prophet's words and patriarchal blessing.) Slide arrow back and forth to tune into the Lord's will and receive guidance throughout life.

RIGHTEOUS RADIO

I will tune into the Lord's will each day as I kneel beside my bed in PRAYER.

I will STUDY AND MEDITATE on the scriptures whenever I can, as I search and ponder the Lord's plan.

The gift of the HOLY GHOST is promised, you see, as I live the commandments, His spirit whispers to me.

I will choose GOOD FRIENDS who help me keep thoughts pure, for Heavenly Father has rewards and rich blessings in store.

BY the PROPHET'S WORDS my actions I will measure, and a PATRIARCHAL BLESSING I will treasure.

CHALLENGE

Make a *"Value"able Tune-In List*, committing to listen only to uplifting music, to watch only uplifting movies and TV shows, and to use only uplifting computer programs or internet sites. Hearing or viewing good media and avoiding bad will help keep us pure. Read D&C 50:2–3 about false spirits who deceive. We can become vulnerable to Satan's power if we listen to his lies. Remember that music, movies, and other media with bad values may entice us with the "glitter of a good time," as Elder Dallin H. Oaks called it ("Be Not Deceived," *Ensign,* Nov. 2004).

TREATS

Graham-cracker Radio. To represent tuner and volume knobs, place two gumdrops on a frosted graham cracker, one on the left and one on the right. Place five smaller gumdrops or candies across the top to represent the five "radio stations" discussed above. Review the five ways to tune into personal revelation.

MORE LESSON IDEAS: See *Young Women Manual 3,* lesson 7.

#32
ACCOUNTABLE W.O.W. ACTIONS

> **AHEAD OF TIME:** Print *Healthful Food Magnets** (shown) using CD-ROM—codes: 32 (b&w) or 32C (color). To make, cut out food visuals and glue a magnet on the back of each.

SONGS & SCRIPTURE

Sing "Choose the Right Way" and "Quickly I'll Obey" (*Children's Songbook,* 160, 197); read D&C 89:18–21.

SHORT LESSON

We can keep our body sacred by not using the harmful things mentioned in the Word of Wisdom (D&C 89). Accountable W.O.W. (Word of Wisdom) actions can be easy if we focus on what our body needs: healthy food, exercise, and rest. If we concentrate on high-nutrition foods, we will be blessed.

"Plant" some nutritional ideas by talking about a plant that receives little water, little sunlight, and no fertilizer, versus a plant that receives adequate water, sunlight, and fertilizer. Explain that we are made of the same molecules as other living organisms and that our body requires certain nutrients to retain health. Some foods can be poisonous to our bodies and some foods are like medicine to our bodies. It's easy to tell whether or not people properly care for themselves. Those who don't do so tend to look tired and sickly. People who eat right, exercise, and get good sleep usually look happy and energetic.

Eating healthy foods is not a guarantee against illness, but it helps us to be as strong and healthy as possible. Following the Word of Wisdom, practicing good nutrition, and getting regular exercise are all excellent preparations for future missionaries (see *The Presidents of the Church Teacher's Manual,* 63).

*ACTIVITY

Make magnets (shown) to post on the refrigerator to remind you to be accountable for keeping the W.O.W. (Word of Wisdom) by watching what you eat. When you turn *W.O.W.* upside-down, it looks like *M.O.M.,* so listen to Mom's advice on nutrition.

Turn the magnets over and write W.O.W. actions on the back. For example, on the back of the "Go bananas over fruit!" magnet, write: "Make a peanut butter and banana sandwich or fruit salad."

CHALLENGE

Share favorite family food and talk about why it is good for you. During the week, try to eat only healthy food, as Daniel did in the Old Testament (see Daniel 1:8–16). Note that *pulse* (verse 12) means foods made of seeds, grains, etc.

Living in the Babylonian king's court in their youth, Daniel and his friends would not eat the king's meat (rich food) or drink his wine, since they knew it was not good for them. Because of this, they grew strong and healthy and were blessed with wisdom. We are promised blessings of wisdom, even "hidden treasures of knowledge" for keeping the Word of Wisdom today (D&C 89:19). See also Mosiah 9:8–9; D&C 89:14.

TREATS

Serving Up Nutrition. Serve seeds, corn, grains, fruits, vegetables, whole-grain muffins, or cornbread with honey. Have a discussion about the benefits of whatever treat you select.

MORE LESSON IDEAS: See *Young Women Manual 1,* lesson 38.

#33

WORD OF WISDOM

> *AHEAD OF TIME:* Print *Word of Wisdom Voting Ballot** (shown) using CD-ROM—codes: 33 (b&w) or 33C (color). Read talk by Boyd K. Packer: "The Word of Wisdom: The Principle and the Promises," *Ensign,* May 1996 (see www.lds.org/library).

SONGS & SCRIPTURE

Sing "For Health and Strength" and "The Word of Wisdom" (*Children's Songbook,* 20, 154); read D&C 89:2.

SHORT LESSON

If we say "yes" to the Word of Wisdom, the Lord's law of health, we will find "wisdom and great treasures of knowledge, even hidden treasures" (D&C 89:19). Tell the story by Boyd K. Packer of a king who wanted to hire a new driver for his coach. The king decided to choose the driver who stayed "on the safe side of things" rather than the one who got close to the edge of the cliff (see "Ahead of Time" above). Compare this story to following the Word of Wisdom.

Satan tries to trick us into believing that harmful substances—such as tobacco, liquor, tea, coffee, and illegal drugs—will do us no harm. He also tries to convince us that overeating and overindulging will not hurt us. He wants us to go along with the crowd, to "be a good sport," so that we will acquire bad habits that will harm our health.

Saying "no" to the substances that are against the Word of Wisdom will bring us blessings. The gospel teaches us that our body, mind, and spirit are connected and are affected by what we take into our body. When we follow the Lord's law of health, we help keep our body healthy, and we are promised wisdom and knowledge (see D&C 89:18–21).

65

*ACTIVITY

What is healthful and what is harmful to my body? Fill in the *Word of Wisdom Voting Ballot* (shown) by looking up the scriptures and then voting "No" to harmful things and "Yes" to good things by checking the column next to the statement.

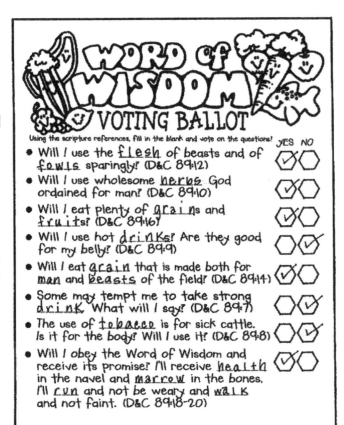

WORD of WISDOM VOTING BALLOT

Using the scripture references, fill in the blank and vote on the questions!

YES NO

- Will I use the f l e s h of beasts and of f o w l s sparingly? (D&C 89:12) ☑ ⬡
- Will I use wholesome h e r b s God ordained for man? (D&C 89:10) ☑ ⬡
- Will I eat plenty of g r a i ns and f r u i t s? (D&C 89:16) ☑ ⬡
- Will I use hot d r i n k s? Are they good for my belly? (D&C 89:9) ⬡ ☑
- Will I eat g r a i n that is made both for man and b e a s t s of the field? (D&C 89:14) ☑ ⬡
- Some may tempt me to take strong d r i n k. What will I say? (D&C 89:7) ⬡ ☑
- The use of t o b a c c o is for sick cattle. Is it for the body? Will I use it? (D&C 89:8) ⬡ ☑
- Will I obey the Word of Wisdom and receive its promise? I'll receive h e a l t h in the navel and m a r r o w in the bones. I'll r u n and not be weary and w a l k and not faint. (D&C 89:18-20) ☑ ⬡

CHALLENGE

Encourage other family members to keep the Word of Wisdom, and look forward to receiving the blessings of keeping it. Talk about the special promise found in D&C 89:18–21.

TREATS

Healthful Choice Food. Provide several different healthful foods, such as a platter of raw fruit and vegetables. Talk about the variety of healthful foods we can choose from. Before eating the food, be sure to bless it and thank Heavenly Father for the healthful choices we have and for revealing the Word of Wisdom through the Prophet Joseph Smith.

MORE LESSON IDEAS: See *Primary D&C Manual 5,* lesson 24.

#34
NEAT & MODEST APPEARANCE

AHEAD OF TIME: Print *Time for a Change Diaper Bag* and cards* (shown) using CD-ROM—codes: 34a and 34b (b&w), or 34aC and 34bC (color). To make, cut out and fold in center, then glue back-to-back on bottom-left and bottom-right sides only, leaving top open.

SONGS & SCRIPTURE

Sing "I'm Trying to Be Like Jesus" and "The Commandments" (*Children's Songbook,* 78, 112); read 1 Timothy 2:9.

SHORT LESSON

Your body is one of Heavenly Father's greatest gifts to you. Besides keeping the Word of Wisdom (D&C 89), there are three ways we can show thanks and take care of our bodies. As we do these things, we invite the companionship of the Holy Ghost and can be a good influence on other people.

1. *Wear Modest Clothing.* We should always dress modestly to show respect for God and ourselves. No matter what the occasion, we should maintain our dress standards. In the *For the Strength of Youth* booklet, we learn that we should avoid clothes that are too tight, revealing (such as too short or too low cut), or extreme in style. If we're not sure whether something is modest or not, we can ask ourselves how we would feel wearing that clothing in the presence of the Lord (see *For the Strength of Youth,* 15-16).

2. *Have a Clean Appearance.* Having a neat and clean appearance will lift our minds and increase our confidence. Spencer W. Kimball said, "Some young people have prided themselves in wearing the most tattered, soiled, and grubby attire. If we dress in a shabby or sloppy manner, we tend to think and act the same way. I am positive that personal grooming and cleanliness, as well as the clothes we wear, can be tremendous factors in the standards we set and follow on the pathway to immortality and eternal life" (*The Teachings of Spencer W. Kimball,* 380).

3. *Not Disfigure My Body.* "The temple of God is holy, which temple ye are" (1 Corinthians 3:17). President Gordon B. Hinckley has urged us to respect our bodies and not inflict permanent damage on them with tattoos and body piercings, reminding us that "the temple of God is holy, which temple ye are" (1 Corinthians 3:17). (See also "When Thou Art Converted,"LDS Library, 2006; Gordon B. Hinckley, "Great Shall Be the Peace of Thy Children," *Ensign,* Nov. 2000. (As stated, no position was taken on "the minimal piercing of the ears by women for one pair of earrings.")

*ACTIVITY

Fill out the cards, following instructions on back. Then place cards in "diaper." If you follow these guidelines, you can "change."

CHALLENGE

With your parents, go through your closet and decide which items can be worn alone, and which need to be layered to create a modest look. Discard those items that are too tight, too short, or otherwise immodest. Ask yourself, "If I were to design clothing for Latter-day Saints, what would it look like?" Go through a fashion magazine or pattern book and redesign the clothing to make it modest, drawing with markers the modest line of dress following guidelines on "diaper" (above).

TREATS

Modest Fashion Cookies. Cut modest clothing shapes out of sugar cookie dough. Frost them according to your personal fashion sense.

#35

DRESS MODESTLY TO STAY CHASTE

> **AHEAD OF TIME:** Print *Temple Light Poster* * (shown) using
> CD-ROM—code: 35 (b&w).

SONGS & SCRIPTURE

Sing "I Love to See the Temple" and "Keep the Commandments" (*Children's Songbook*, 95, 146); read Jacob 2:28.

SHORT LESSON

When we dress modestly, showing respect for Heavenly Father and ourselves, it is easier to live the law of chastity. The decisions we make early in life will prepare us so that we can have a celestial marriage, to be sealed to our chosen companion in the temple for time and eternity.

President Spencer W. Kimball said, "The [decisions] are of two kinds: 'This I *will do*' and 'This I *will not do.*'" . . . "Very early, youth should have been living by a plan. . . . [They should] set a course in their education, a mission, the finding of a pure, clean sweetheart to be a life's companion, their temple marriage and their Church service. When such a course is charted and the goal is set, it is easier to resist the many temptations and to say 'no' to the first cigarette, 'no' to the first drink. . . . 'no' to . . . immoral [unvirtuous] practices" (*The Miracle of Forgiveness*, 236).

Modest dress shows that we respect our body as a temple. Our body houses our eternal spirit and—when we're worthy—the Holy Ghost (see 1 Corinthians 3:16–17). Modest dress can protect us from physical, emotional, and spiritual harm. Heavenly Father wants us to be modest to help us to be chaste—to reserve physical intimacy for marriage.

(For more information about teaching chastity in your home, see "Talking with Your Children about Moral Purity," *Ensign*, Dec. 1986.)

ACTIVITY

As a reminder to live the law of chastity, family can punch pinholes in this backwards picture. When they place it in a window (facing out), they can read the message on the other side as the light shines through the pinholes.

CHALLENGE

Set goals to accomplish in life that will help you live worthy to marry in the temple, starting with the *Gospel Standards*. Examples: dress modestly; use clean words; watch and read uplifting and wholesome movies, television programs, videos, books, and magazines; listen to uplifting music and songs; keep body pure; obey the Word of Wisdom; think pure thoughts; choose good friends; do not date until age 16.

TREATS

Temple-worthy Waffles. Make waffles, topping with butter, cinnamon, and sugar if desired. Tell family these waffles represent the strait and narrow path to the temple. When we slip off the path (into the waffle hole) by doing something wrong, we need to repent and promise not to commit the sin again. We can then get back on the path and keep the commandments so we are worthy to go to the temple when the time comes.

MORE LESSON IDEAS: See *Primary D&C Manual 5*, lesson 44.

#36

PRAISEWORTHY ENTERTAINMENT

> **AHEAD OF TIME:** Print *TV Topper and Bookshelf Buddy** (shown) using CD-ROM—codes: 36 (b&w) or 36C (color). To make, cut out, cutting a slit at the bottom, then folding and inserting the tab in the slit.

SONGS & SCRIPTURE

Sing "Listen, Listen" and "Stand for the Right" (*Children's Songbook,* 107, 159); read Alma 53:20.

SHORT LESSON

President Gordon B. Hinckley has counseled us not to waste our time on pointless activities. He explains that spending time on activities that don't teach us anything doesn't leave us time to do more important things (see "Gambling," *Ensign,* May 2005). If we watch and read only things that Jesus or the prophet would watch or read, we are participating in praiseworthy entertainment. In 1 Corinthians 3:16–17 we read, "Know ye not that ye are the temple of God, and that the Spirit of God dwelleth in you? If any man defile the temple of God, him shall God destroy; for the temple of God is holy, which temple ye are."

Ponder the poster found in the February 2002 *New Era* (p. 19), showing an ice cream sundae with whipped cream and a cherry on top and an ugly cockroach climbing out of the middle. The poster says, "It's great except for the bad parts. What kinds of movies and music are you feeding your mind?" (You can find the *New Era* at www.lds.org, Gospel Library— Magazines.)

*ACTIVITY

How can we judge the right things to read and watch? Create the *TV Topper* and *Bookshelf Buddy* (shown right), which you can place on your television or bookshelf as a reminder to choose worthy TV shows, movies, books, and magazines. Read and memorize the quotes to help avoid worldly media influences.

CHALLENGE

In the next few weeks during TV commercials, read to your family about how we can make appropriate media choices. For example, see Joseph Walker's article titled "Reel Life vs. Real Life" (*Ensign,* June 1993). Walker, a professional TV

critic, says that "reel" life (reality as portrayed by movies and TV shows) is frequently far removed from actual reality, especially for people trying to follow God's commandments. (Another good resource is "A Conversation on Things of the Spirit, Pornography, and Certain Kinds of Movies, Books, and Magazines," *New Era,* May 1971.)

TREATS

Questionable Brownies.

1. Prepare brownies ahead of time and divide them on to two separate plates. Attach a note to one plate that reads "Questionable Brownies."
2. With the two plates of brownies in front of family, talk about movies, Hollywood standards, movie ratings, etc. Consider phrases that people might use after going to movies (e.g., "There's only a little swearing," "Just a few dirty jokes," "You didn't see much," or "I've seen worse").
3. Tell family you made some brownies with the best ingredients. Then hold up the plate with the Questionable Brownies sign and say, "What if I told you that I added a little bit of doggie doo-doo to this batch? 'Just a little never hurt anyone. Try them!' What would you do?" After getting their reaction, explain, "These are completely edible. There's really no doggie doo-doo in them." Eat one yourself as you hand out the rest.
4. While you enjoy the brownies, read 2 Nephi 28:21. Talk about ways Satan leads people "carefully down to hell," by adding just a little here and there through desensitization. Resolve that before participating in media, you will ask yourself, "Do I like doggie doo-doo in my brownies?"

MORE LESSON IDEAS: See *Young Women Manual 1,* lesson 33.

#37

SCRIPTURE BLESSINGS

AHEAD OF TIME: Print *Scripture Blessings Sticker Challenge** (shown) using CD-ROM—codes: 37a and 37b (b&w), or 37aC and 37bC (color). To make, cut out the glue-on stickers, and store near the reading chart.

SONGS & SCRIPTURE

Sing "Seek the Lord Early" and "Search, Ponder, and Pray" (*Children's Songbook,* 108, 109); read 2 Timothy 3:15.

SHORT LESSON

It is hard for us to remember things that happened long ago unless we read about them often. We read family journals and look at scrapbooks and photo albums to remember our family, but do we remember the counsel we received in heaven before we were born? Heavenly Father and Jesus are pleased when we read the scriptures and learn of Their plan for us. The Ten Commandments, given by Jesus to the prophet Moses thousands of years ago, are still in force in our time, along with other teachings of Jesus and His prophets. In Isaiah 40:8, we read, "The grass withereth, the flower fadeth: but the word of our God shall stand for ever."

Article of Faith 8 says, "We believe the Bible to be the word of God as far as it is translated correctly; we also believe the Book of Mormon to be the word of God." Through the power of God, Joseph Smith translated the Bible, fixing the mistakes in the book. We receive many blessings from reading the scriptures. Not only do they direct us and teach us, but they also give us hope. Romans 15:4 reads, "For whatsoever things were written aforetime were written for our learning, that we through patience and comfort of the scriptures might have hope."

73

Elder John A. Widtsoe said that a righteous student who spends even ten minutes a day studying the gospel will be blessed with an increase in both faith and knowledge of his school subjects (see *Evidences & Reconciliations*, 42).

ACTIVITY

Do the *Scripture Blessings Sticker Challenge* (shown) to learn the importance of reading the scriptures and to learn the blessings that come from reading the scriptures and keeping the commandments.
To Do: Read the two scriptures for each day starting with Sunday. Decide which scripture tells you to read the scriptures and which scripture tells you the blessings that come from reading the scriptures and obeying the commandments.
Glue a "Read!" or a "Blessing!" sticker to the right of each scripture (see answers above).

CHALLENGE

Share with each other your feelings about the great blessings the scriptures bring to your life. Tell about the joy and peace they bring as you remember to obey Heavenly Father's laws. Study the scriptures together each day this week and talk about your impressions.

TREATS

Standard Works Cookies. For each family member, break one four-piece graham cracker into four pieces. Frost each piece, then stack them. Tell family that the scriptures consist of the four standard works: the Bible, Book of Mormon, Doctrine and Covenants, and Pearl of Great Price. Discuss how these books of scripture differ from each other.

MORE LESSON IDEAS: See *Primary Old Testament Manual 6*, lesson 37.

#38

"BEE" SMART READING CHOICES

Ahead of Time: Print *"Bee" Smart Bookmark* and *Smart Bees and Hearts Checkers** (shown) using CD-ROM—codes: 38a, 38b, 38c, and 38d (b&w); or 38aC, 38bC, 38cC, and 38dC (color). To make, cut out bookmark, checkerboard, and hearts and bees checkers. Fold bookmark and glue back-to-back.

SONGS & SCRIPTURE

Sing "Search, Ponder, and Pray" and "A Young Man Prepared" (*Children's Songbook,* 109, 166); read 1 Timothy 4:13.

SHORT LESSON

We can "bee" smart by improving our study habits and choosing wholesome books that will uplift our mind and spirit.

President Gordon B. Hinckley challenged the youth to "be smart" and "be clean" ("A Prophet's Counsel and Prayer for Youth," *Ensign,* Jan. 2001). Reading is important because it helps us learn, but we must be careful to avoid reading material that discourages the companionship of the Holy Ghost.

Many good books and magazines are available. Reading is a great way to spend our time, a great way to occupy our mind and imagination, and we will probably never run out of new and interesting choices. (See also Gordon B. Hinckley, "Gambling," *Ensign,* May 2005.)

To develop wholesome reading habits, we can (1) tune out the world, e.g., television and reading material that does not invite the Spirit, and (2) tune into things of the Spirit that invite pure thoughts, e.g. scriptures, Church magazines, and reading recommended to us by trusted sources, such as our parents.

*ACTIVITY

1. Create a *"Bee" Smart Bookmark* to help you make wholesome reading choices. On the back of *Bookmark,* write titles of good books you want to read and books you love.
2. Play *Smart Bees and Hearts Checkers* by following the instructions on the game.

CHALLENGE

Talk to your family about improving study habits. One wholesome reading habit is to read the scriptures each day. Howard W. Hunter taught that studying the scriptures can remind us how often Heavenly Father promises blessings for His

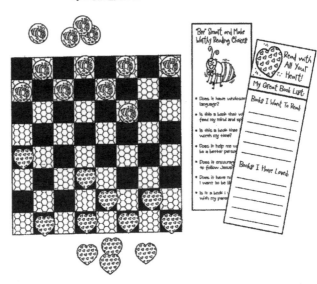

people's obedience. (See "Commitment to God," *Ensign,* Nov. 1982.)

TREATS

Honey "Bee" Smart Taffy. Make honey taffy to remind you to work hard to get an education so you can "bee" better mothers and fathers and provide for your own families someday. We can follow the example of the busy bees, who work all day carrying pollen and nectar from flowers to their hive. Let's "bee" smart and work hard.

To Make Taffy: In a 6" deep saucepan, boil 1 cup of honey for 7 to 10 minutes on medium-high heat, cooking to a soft-ball stage. Test by dropping one-half teaspoon honey into cold water. If you can form it into a round ball with your fingers, it's done. Pour onto a buttered cutting board (marble or plastic), and cool 5 minutes. Then pull and stretch the honey into taffy, adding butter as you pull. Form and cut into bite-size pieces.

#39
"NOTE" WORTHY SONGS

> **Ahead of Time:** Print *Band Concert Instrument* labels* (shown) using CD-ROM—codes: 39 (b&w) or 39C (color). To make, cut out shaker and tambourine labels, then glue them on a paper plate and cup. Place a handful of rice, unpopped popcorn, or beans on another paper plate and in another cup. Seal two plates by punching holes and threading yarn snugly through holes; tape two cups to seal.

SONGS & SCRIPTURE

Sing "Hum Your Favorite Hymn" and "Sing Your Way Home" (*Children's Songbook,* 152, 193); read D&C 25:12–13.

SHORT LESSON

If a song is "note"worthy it is pleasing to Heavenly Father. If we only listen to music that pleases Him, we will be happy. Certain music and songs are not pleasing to Heavenly Father. If we learn the Primary songs and Church hymns, we can get a good idea of the types of songs we should be listening to and singing. President Joseph Fielding Smith said, "Good music is gracious praise of the Lord. It is delightsome to the ear, and it is one of our most acceptable methods of worshiping" (*Conference Report,* Oct. 1969).

As a family, choose a favorite Church hymn or reverent Primary song, e.g., "I Am a Child of God." Talk about the uplifting words and music and how it makes you feel happy and inspired. Review the song carefully and memorize it. (See Boyd K. Packer, "Inspiring Music—Worthy Thoughts," *Ensign,* Jan. 1974.)

Ask yourself, Is the song "note"worthy? Does it offer to Heavenly Father "praise and thanksgiving" (D&C 136:28)? Does it help you think of things praiseworthy (Article of Faith 13)? If so, seek after it.

Sing together in family home evenings, and sing to cheer someone up. The mood of the household can quickly be lifted by singing together, and many happy memories can be created. Sing any time of the day in your home. If you sing first thing in the morning, you start the day happy.

*ACTIVITY

Strike up a band with the *Concert Instruments* (shown), and sing the "Happy Song" (*Children's Songbook*, 264), illustrated on the tambourine (shown right) as follows: "Ducks in the pond quack a happy song. Mother hens cackle the whole day long. Birds in their nests and wind in the treetops, All join in singing a happy song. Children are singing a happy song, Singing together the whole day long. Don't mind the weather; let's sing together, All join in singing a happy song." Shake instruments and help children march. (Visit www.lds.org to play music.)

CHALLENGE

Talk to family about songs that help us to be righteous, songs that bring the Spirit and help us think of spiritual things. These are songs we should sing often in family home evening, in church, and in our hearts. Have family members name their favorite songs. Play songs from the *Children's Songbook* and the hymn book (*Hymns*) that the family is familiar with to see if they can guess the tunes.

TREATS

Sunbeam Cookies. Eat smile-frosted cookies and sing "Jesus Wants Me for a Sunbeam" (*Children's Songbook*, 60).

MORE LESSON IDEAS: See *Primary Nursery Manual 1,* lesson 39.

#40
UPLIFTING MUSIC & SONGS

AHEAD OF TIME: Print *Celestial Singing Meter**(shown) using CD-ROM —codes: 40a, 40b, and 40c (b&w); or 40aC, 40bC and 40cC (color). To make, cut out and mount the two-part chart on posterboard and laminate the entire poster, or display chart on a magnetic board or cork board. Write the songs you want to practice on the stars, then laminate and cut out stars (laminate stars *before* writing the song titles if you want to use erasable markers to change the songs over time).

SONGS & SCRIPTURE

Sing "Lift Up Your Voice and Sing" and "Sing a Song"(*Children's Songbook*, 252, 253); read Ephesians 5:19.

SHORT LESSON

A good way to decide if music or lyrics are pleasing to the Lord is to ask yourself if they invite celestial thoughts.

Elder Ezra Taft Benson, who later became President of the Church, warned us against "the demoralizing, loud, raucous beat of rock music, which deadens the senses and dulls the sensibilities—the jungle rhythm which inflames the savagery within" (*Conference Report,* Oct. 1970).

Elder George P. Lee of the Seventy counseled us to avoid worshiping hard rock music and other worldly idols, which he says results in "holding hands with Satan and . . . walking in darkness." Elder Lee explained that if we neglect the spiritual in favor of worldly music or the rock stars that produce it, we are worshiping idols. This idolatry will deaden our spiritual senses, and we will become less interested in church and in service to God. Our minds will be overshadowed by fears, and we will stray from God's path. To stay in the light, we must turn away from these idols. (See "Staying Unspotted from the World," *Ensign,* May 1978.)

While chairman of the Church Youth Music Committee, Larry Bastian explained that uplifting and ennobling songs can be classified as "good music," but songs that merely entertain or brighten our mood can also be useful. We should always avoid, however, any music that makes us think unrighteous thoughts. (See "I Have a Question," *Ensign,* July 1974.)

*ACTIVITY

Have a "celestial singers" practice to see if you can become the best. Write titles of songs you want to sing, then tape them on the back or front of the stars. Each time you practice singing, have someone judge whether the song should be moved up or down on the chart. The brightness of your singing reflects the brightness of the kingdoms. With each song, your goal is to make it to the celestial kingdom. If you need to practice more, leave the stars in place until next time.

Talk about the three degrees of glory. Explain how happy we will be when we reach the celestial kingdom, because we can live there forever with Heavenly Father, Jesus Christ, and our families (D&C 76:62).

CHALLENGE

Spend time singing uplifting songs, so that when you need to be lifted spiritually you can hum the melody or think the words. Songs can be the same ones you sing each week in family home evening. Pick your favorites to put on the stars, so you can be celestial singers.

TREATS

Star or Music-note Cookies. With cookie cutters, cut out sugar cookies in the shape of stars or musical notes. Bake, frost, and enjoy the cookies while listening to beautiful music or your favorite songs.

#41

HUM RIGHTEOUS THOUGHTS

AHEAD OF TIME: Print *Hum a Hymn Hummingbird Poster** (shown) using CD-ROM——codes: 41 (b&w) or 41C (color).

SONGS & SCRIPTURE

Sing "Hum Your Favorite Hymn" and "Lift Up Your Voice and Sing" (*Children's Songbook.* 152, 252); read Psalm 69:30.

SHORT LESSON

As we learn to sing Primary songs and Church hymns, we can think about them anytime to replace unwholesome thoughts. By choosing a favorite hymn or two, we can change our attitude and our mind. (See Boyd K. Packer, *That All May Be Edified,* 101; see also David B. Haight, "Be a Strong Link," *Ensign,* Nov. 2000.)

President Gordon B. Hinckley warned against unwholesome entertainers who are very popular but whose songs have suggestive themes (see "An Ensign to the Nations, a Light to the World," *Ensign,* Nov. 2003).

LDS musician Duane E. Hiatt wrote, "Music also has great power. Many years ago in Massachusetts, Elder Boyd K. Packer advised a group of us that when we are discouraged or downcast or tempted to do evil, we can think of our mind as a stage. Little actors come out on that stage to give our minds certain messages. If these are not the thoughts and feelings we want to hold, there is an easy way to sweep the stage and bring on better actors. 'Just hum your favorite hymn,' Elder Packer said, 'and it will drive those bad actors off the stage of your mind and bring on the good actors'" (see Duane E. Hiatt, *Overcoming Personal Loss,* 31–2).

*ACTIVITY

Tell family that we can be just as quick as a hummingbird that flaps its wings, to replace unwholesome thoughts. They are the smallest birds in the world (3-6 inches tall). Hummingbirds get their name from the humming sound made by their wings, which flap 60 to 70 times per second. (See http://en.wikipedia.org/wiki/Hummingbird for information and photos.) Think about how quick we can be at humming our favorite tune or thinking a wholesome thought when needed. Select a hymn or Primary song and write it on the poster (shown), then memorize the words to be ready when you need wholesome thoughts to replace unwholesome thoughts to "Let virtue garnish thy thoughts unceasingly" (D&C 121:45).

CHALLENGE

Choose a weapon to fight immoral thoughts by memorizing a wholesome poem, song, hymn, thought, or impression of a picture. Have some inspirational music, poetry, paintings, etc., on hand to share. Hang a painting of the Savior in your home. Discuss these inspirational things, and enjoy them together. Express your love and concern for family members, explaining how you want them to be protected from the evils of the world.

TREATS

Sweet Humming. Offer sips from a fruit smoothie or milkshake as rewards for the following: Have family members take turns coming up and humming a line or two of their favorite hymn. If another family member guesses the hymn within 15 seconds, give him or her a sip of the smoothie or shake. Also give the hummer a sip for participating.

More Lesson Ideas: See *Young Women Manual 1*, lesson 34.

#42

LOVE OTHERS

Ahead of Time: Print *Spiral Love Kite** (shown) using CD-ROM—codes: 42 (b&w) or 42C (color). To make, cut out, punch a hole at the top, and tie on a yarn or ribbon for the kite string.

SONGS & SCRIPTURE

Sing "Jesus Said Love Everyone" and "I'm Trying to Be like Jesus" (*Children's Songbook,* 61, 78); read John 13:34.

SHORT LESSON

We can follow Jesus Christ by keeping all of His commandments. One of His greatest commandments is to love one another.

In Matthew 22:37–39, Jesus commands us to love God with all our heart and to love our neighbor as we love ourselves. Who are our neighbors? Our neighbors are our family members, friends, and everyone else who needs our love. In Mosiah 23:15, we learn that Alma taught his people that "every man should love his neighbor as himself, that there should be no contention among them." Discuss ways, both big and small, that the world would be different if everyone tried to follow this teaching.

When we show love for others, we are showing charity, "the pure love of Christ" (Moroni 7:47). Jesus Christ loved us so much that He was willing to suffer for our sins and die for us. Read 2 Nephi 26:30; Ether 12:33–34; 1 John 3:16; John 15:13.

Read the *Spiral Love Kite* (shown) to learn ways we can love others: being kind to others, speaking kind words, saying "please" and "thank you," helping others, smiling at everyone, and following Jesus. We can make our home a heaven on earth by loving others as directed by Jesus and His prophets. If we do, our love at home will increase.

*ACTIVITY

For younger children, create and parade the *Spiral Love Kite* (shown), sharing ways you can love others (listed on the kite). Bounce and twirl kite as you smile, knowing you now know many ways to love others.

CHALLENGE

Talk about the ways you want to show love to your family members. As you practice on them, it will be easier to show love to those outside your family. Talk about ways we can be of service to our neighbors, e.g., visiting the elderly to cheer them up.

Ideas: Take your elderly neighbors some healthy treats, help make your brother's bed, set the table for Mother, play with the baby, greet Dad when he comes home, get your homework done early so you can help younger brothers and sisters with theirs, save money to buy birthday and Christmas gifts for others.

TREATS

Heart-shaped Cookie. Talk about ten ways you can show love that are not on the *Spiral Love Kite*, e.g.: do a good deed; share what you like about a person; say, "good job"; ask how you can help someone; listen carefully to others; share your things with those who have less; mend a quarrel; forgive someone who has hurt you; invite a new person to join you and your friends; give a heartfelt gift; share a treat; find out someone's interests and learn about things they like.

MORE LESSON IDEAS: See *Primary Nursery Manual 1,* lesson 34.

#43

SERVE OTHERS

AHEAD OF TIME: Print *Good Samaritan Scene** (shown) using CD-ROM—codes: 43 (b&w) or 43C (color). To make, attach arm with a paper fastener and paste story on back.

SONGS & SCRIPTURE

Sing "I Will Be Valiant" and "Go the Second Mile" (*Children's Songbook,* 162, 167); read D&C 4:2.

SHORT LESSON

We can serve others by treating them kindly and helping with their needs. Service could be a simple smile, a compliment, or lending a helping hand. We should all serve others because we are so blessed, and because the Lord has commanded us to serve. When we serve others, we are serving Heavenly Father and Jesus Christ. In Mosiah 2:17, we learn that "when [we] are in the service of [our] fellow beings [we] are only in the service of [our] God."

We can serve others by giving. For example, with the children's help, Mother could make dinner, bread, or a dessert for someone in need. This might be a sister in the ward with a new baby, a friend who has lost a loved one, or an elderly neighbor who is ill. The whole family can write a nice note to the person in need, then deliver it with the food.

Start service in the family, for it is a classroom where we can apply "charity . . . patience, sharing, integrity, kindness, generosity, self-control, and service" (see "A Balm in Gilead," *Ensign,* Nov. 1995).

*ACTIVITY

Heavenly Father wants us to show love to others through service. Using the *Good Samaritan Scene* (shown), tell the story in Luke 10:30–37, moving the hand holding the cup up and down to give the man a drink. This parable, plus many of Jesus' other parables (found in the New Testament),

I can serve others.

other scriptures, and Church magazine stories and articles, contain suggestions to prepare us to help and serve others.

CHALLENGE

As a family, think of and talk about someone you can help, and what specifically you will do. Know that sometimes the people you serve won't thank you, and that you may never know if your service is appreciated or not. But we must serve unconditionally, without hoping for praise. At her husband's funeral, a woman saw her former bishop and said, "I knew you would come." Why did she know he would be there? Because he had loved and served her family for years. (See talk by Elder Marion D. Hanks, *Ensign,* Nov. 1970.)

TREATS

Smiling Face Jell-O (to remind you to always serve with a smile). To make, stir 6 ounces flavored gelatin into 2 ½ cups boiling water. Pour about 1 ½ inches into bowls, then refrigerate 1 hour. Top with whipped cream in the shape of a smile. As you eat, think of the cup that the good Samaritan may have used to give water to and bring a smile to the man that had been beaten and left at the side of the road.

MORE LESSON IDEAS: See *Primary Nursery Manual 1,* lesson 34.

#44

JOY IN SERVICE

AHEAD OF TIME: Print *Serve with Style Match Game** (shown) using CD-ROM—codes: 44a and 44b (b&w) or 44aC and 44bC (color). To make, mount on card stock and cut out.

SONGS & SCRIPTURE

Sing "Go the Second Mile" and "Give Said the Little Stream" (*Children's Songbook, 167, 236*); read Acts 20:35.

SHORT LESSON

We can feel joy and happiness as we serve others. The handcart pioneers were wonderful examples of service. On their way across the plains to Utah, they planted gardens they would never eat from and fruit trees they would never sit under or harvest. M. Russell Ballard told us to never forget the "spirit of sacrifice" the pioneers demonstrated, and to follow in their footsteps. Even in difficult circumstances, we can find happiness and peace by serving others (see "The Blessings of Sacrifice," *Ensign,* May 1992).

Jesus said that when we serve, we find ourselves: "He that findeth his life shall lose it: and he that loseth his life for my sake shall find it" (Matthew 10:39). Service improves the quality of two lives—the giver's and the receiver's. Remember that one of the best ways we can serve others is to pray for them when they are ill or having a hard time.

We should strive to do daily acts of service, such as visiting a homebound friend, testifying of truth to a nonmember, giving food or clothing to those who need it, listening to a friend who needs to talk, asking someone how you can help and then doing it, playing with your siblings while your mother rests, washing and drying the dishes after a meal.

* ACTIVITY

This *Serve with Style Match Game* helps develop an attitude of service. The cards can be posted on a mirror to motivate family members during the week. Introduce game by reading the cards as a matched set, e.g., "You can be fashionable without spending a dime" (card 1) "and serve with a smile time after time" (card 2). Read 2 Corinthians 9:7, then play the game. *To Play:*

Divide into teams and sit in a circle around a table. Lay cards facedown on the table. Take turns drawing a card to make a match.

CHALLENGE

Drive the family around your neighborhood or town. Assign someone to write down everything that could be a service project, with all children calling out ideas. (If the ideas are theirs, they will get excited about service.) Decide which project is needed most and start with that one, planning it and making assignments. Then move on to the next.

TREATS

Fashionable Service Cookies. Cut out sugar cookie dough into fashion shapes like those listed on the cards (shown). As you frost and eat the cookies, talk about the types of service found on the cards. Talk about how you will create a life"style" of service by looking for opportunities to serve on a regular basis. For example, make a weekly visit to a friend you want to serve, perhaps taking them a treat, going for a walk with them, or simply talking to them about their needs. You can always find ways to serve in "style."

MORE LESSON IDEAS: See *Young Women Manual 1*, lesson 30.

#45

SHOW LOVING CARE

Ahead of Time: Print *Service Station Sack Label** (shown) using CD-ROM—codes: 45 (b&w) or 45C (color). To make, cut out label and service reminder wordstrips. Glue label on a lunch-size brown paper bag. Place wordstrips in the bag along with tiny treats for each service.

SONGS & SCRIPTURE

Sing "Shine On" and "A Special Gift Is Kindness" (*Children's Songbook*, 144, 145); read Mark 10:14–16.

SHORT LESSON

It is easy to serve someone you care about or someone who has served you. But when you serve people you don't know well, you learn to care about them too. How can we best serve others?

1. Pray to know whom to serve, then listen to the Holy Ghost (James 1:15).
2. Do things that invite the Holy Ghost, avoiding worldly influences so you will hear the still small voice prompt you (Titus 2:12).
3. Do the things that the Holy Ghost inspires you to do (1 Nephi 3:7).
4. Show service through good deeds. Good deeds start with good thoughts (Mosiah 4:30).
5. Begin service at home, where you can learn to serve one another and feel what it is like to be served (Mosiah 5:13).
6. Love your neighbor as you love yourself (Mosiah 23:15).
7. Follow Jesus' example to lose yourself in the service of others by thinking more of them than yourself, then caring for their needs (Matthew 25:40).

*Activity

Reading the *Service Station Sack Label,* say: "You're at the Service Station! Gas up, take off and help those you 'car'e about."

Have family members add the wordstrips and other service ideas to the sack.

Talk about the rewards that come from service (e.g., feeling happy because we served, increasing our talents, and receiving blessings from Heavenly Father). Then reach into the bag and pull out acts of kindness to do each day or week.

CHALLENGE

Talk about ways you can serve each other, no matter if you are the parent or the child. Talk about King Benjamin in the Book of Mormon, who taught his people to serve each other and how to be happy. He taught them by example, actually serving them instead of just asking them to serve: "Behold, ye have called me your king; and if I, whom ye call your king, do labor to serve you, then ought not ye to labor to serve one another?" (Mosiah 2:18).

TREATS

Life Savers Candy Cars. Give each person a roll of Life Savers candies to use for the car body. Glue four individual Life Savers on the sides of the roll to look like tires. Remind family that if they speed by others, not stopping to serve, they could swerve off the strait and narrow path that leads back to our Heavenly Father.

MORE LESSON IDEAS: See *Primary D&C Manual 5,* lesson 39.

#46

SAY "NO" TO PEER PRESSURE

AHEAD OF TIME: Print *Peer Pressure Cross-Match Puzzle** (shown) using CD-ROM—codes: 46 (b&w) or 46C (color).

SONGS & SCRIPTURE

Sing "I'm Trying to Be Like Jesus" and "Dare to Do Right" (*Children's Songbook,* 78, 158); read D&C 20:22.

SHORT LESSON

True friends should expect and encourage you to obey all the Lord's commandments, and would never ask you to do something wrong. However, some friends might try to get you to do things that Heavenly Father and Jesus would not want you to do. How can we seek good friends and say "no" to negative peer pressure?

1. Don't do something that you know is wrong, even if you're afraid someone won't like you for not doing what he or she asks. It is more important to be trusted than to be liked (see D&C 10:6; 124:20).
2. Be prepared to face temptation by putting on the "whole armour of God" (Ephesians 6:11,13).
3. Pray for the person who is pressuring you to make poor choices (3 Nephi 12:44).
4. Ask a parent or Church leader to help you decide what to do.
5. Do not take even one step down the wrong path. Do not take the first drink, smoke the first cigarette, try a drug once, or look at pornography—ever. Curiosity can bring addiction, which is very difficult to break (2 Ne 31:18-19).
6. Stop and consider the full consequence for each action; think and plan ahead (see 1 Nephi 10:21).
7. Know that a true friend will set an example in living the gospel. Be a true friend to others (2 Nephi 1:30).

*ACTIVITY

Show the *Peer Pressure Cross-Match Puzzle* (shown). Learn how to respond to peer-pressure situations and to be a positive influence on friends by doing this puzzle. Draw an arrow from a situation (center column) to the peer pressure (left column) that matches it. Then draw an arrow from the situation to what you should say (right column). Talk about consequences for each decision. Use a different color to draw each arrow.

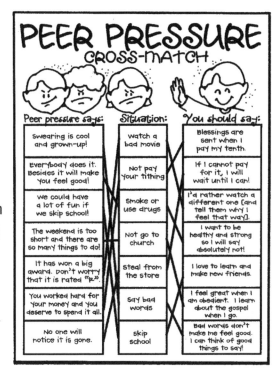

CHALLENGE

Discuss negative peer pressure (from people who want us to do bad things), as well as positive peer pressure (from friends who help us choose the right). We can avoid negative peer pressure by choosing good friends. If we are a good friend to others, we will not ask them to do anything wrong but will influence them with our good example.

TREATS

Peer-pressure Pop. Open a can of soda and talk about the pressure that is released as you lift the lid. Explain that we feel pressure— which makes us uneasy and restless—when friends suggest that we do something bad. We can ease this pressure by knowing our values (what we believe) ahead of time. If we know what is right, we can say "no."

MORE LESSON IDEAS: See *Primary Old Testament Manual 6*, lesson 32.

#47

FORGIVE OTHERS

Ahead of Time: Print *Forgiving Faces Doors** (shown) using CD-ROM—codes: 47a and 47b (b&w), or 47aC and 47bC (color). To make, cut out face situation doors, noting where to glue the numbers. Then glue faces 1 through 4 on the left side of doors as indicated.

SONGS & SCRIPTURE

Sing "Help Me, Dear Father" and "I Will Walk with You" (*Children's Songbook,* 99, 140); read Mosiah 26:30.

SHORT LESSON

If you are a good friend, you will forgive others, but this does not mean that you need to accept their unrighteous actions. How can we seek good friends, treat others kindly, and still stay away from unrighteous situations?

1. Know and live the standards set in For the Strength of Youth, writing these standards into our heart and mind and live accordingly. You will be guided by the Spirit to help you know what to do.
2. Follow the Savior. When crucified, He said, "Father, forgive them; for they know not what they do" (Luke 23:34).
3. Give aid to the weary. President Gordon B. Hinckley said that this world needs us to be strong, virtuous, faithful, and be willing to forgive and forget. He asked us to reach out in friendship to everyone about us. (See "The Need for Greater Kindness," *Conference Report, Ensign,* May 2006).
4. Spread sunshine. When we are unforgiving, we are unkind and mean to others, this adds to this world of selfishness and gloom. Let's give aid to the needy, to the downtrodden, to the weak, and to those who feel hurt and lonely, and inadequate. Let's truly forgive and move on to a new attitude of peace and happiness.

4. Forget ourselves and settle our differences, and we can be filled with the Spirit and know what we can do to obtain joy and happiness. In 3 Nephi 11:29 we learn that the "spirit of contention is not of me (God), but is of the devil, who is the father of contention, and he stirreth up the hears of men to contend with anger, one with another."

5. Follow the golden rule and love our neighbors as ourselves. This will bring great joy and happiness in our lives. When we forgive and love, we can be friends with our Savior, others, and ourselves.

6. Forgive others to be happy. In 3 Nephi 13:14-15 we learn that we are to "forgive men their trespasses" so that our Heavenly Father can forgive us. Loving our neighbors as ourselves will bring joy and happiness.

*ACTIVITY

A good friend would have a forgiving face. With younger children, open the *Forgiving Faces Doors* (shown) to look at and talk about the situations and "forgiving face" responses. Know that you will be happier when you forgive. With older children and teens, talk about doors they face in forgiving friends.

CHALLENGE

Make a list of actions that require forgiveness and what you can do to show forgiveness and love. Read D&C 64:10: "I, the Lord, will forgive whom I will forgive, but of you it is required to forgive all men."

TREATS

Feeling Face Cookies. Frost round cookies and top with dried fruit or candy to make the eyes, nose, and mouth. Tell family that a face can tell us many things, but a forgiving face will have a smile.

MORE LESSON IDEAS: See *Primary CTR-A Manual 2,* lesson 40.

#48

PREPARE TO SHARE THE GOSPEL

AHEAD OF TIME: Print *Missionary Prep Mirror Motivators** (shown) using CD-ROM—codes: 48 (b&w) or 48C (color). Print a set for each family member. To make, cut out.

SONGS & SCRIPTURE

Sing "I Want to Be a Missionary Now" and "We'll Bring the World His Truth" (*Children's Songbook*, 168, 172); read D&C 4:2–3.

SHORT LESSON

Heavenly Father has asked us to share the gospel with others (see D&C 42:12; D&C 88:81). Here are ways you can prepare and share the gospel:

1. *Build Your Testimony.* Attend church each week, listening to the lessons; participate in family home evening; read the scriptures and words of the prophets and leaders in the Church magazines; keep the commandments; and pray to increase your faith in Jesus and His gospel.

2. *Develop Your Talents.* God has given every person unique gifts. Give of your time and talents to build up the kingdom of God on the earth, which is the Church (D&C 4:2). As you sacrifice to build up the Church and spread the gospel, lives can be enriched and hearts changed.

3. *Cultivate Good Manners.* Good manners help put you and others at ease.

4. *Learn Other Languages.* This way you can carry the gospel to the world.

5. *Create a Sharing Home.* Share the gospel with your family through family home evening, and scripture and gospel study. Talk about lessons learned.

6. *Bear Your Testimony.* Share your beliefs about the gospel with your family. You should also write your testimony in your journal, express it in the classroom on Sundays, and bear it in testimony meetings.

*ACTIVITY

Give each family member a set of motivators (shown) to post on their mirror and write how they can prepare to be a missionary.

CHALLENGE

Reading each *Missionary Prep Mirror Motivator,* share ways you can prepare for a mission. Have a lesson on doing laundry, ironing a shirt, or preparing a meal. Another way to prepare for a mission is to learn to work hard and enjoy it. When

President Gordon B. Hinckley felt discouraged on his mission, his father wrote him a letter and said, "Forget yourself and go to work." Elder Hinckley knelt and pledged to devote himself to the Lord's work. (See David F. Evans, "Your Mission Will Change Everything," *Ensign,* May 2006.)

TREATS

Missionary Confidence Cupcakes. Make and frost cupcakes.

Option 1: Give each family member a cupcake topped with a question mark written in frosting. Ask them to brainstorm what they can do to be ready so that when a missionary moment comes, they can share the gospel.

Option 2: Write or type investigator questions on slips of paper, roll them up and wrap in foil, and slip them inside cupcakes before frosting them. When a family member finds a question, he or she can pretend to be an investigator and read the question for the other family members to answer.

MORE LESSON IDEAS: See *Young Women Manual 2,* lesson 19.

#49
GAIN ETERNAL LIFE

> *AHEAD OF TIME:* Print *Puzzled About Eternal Life Word Find**
> (shown) using CD-ROM—codes: 49 (b&w) or 49C (color).

SONGS & SCRIPTURE

Sing "I Feel My Savior's Love" and "Keep the Commandments" (*Children's Songbook,* 74, 147); read 3 Nephi 12:20.

SHORT LESSON

Heavenly Father has a plan for us, and He has promised that everyone who is worthy will have eternal life (D&C 59:23). Eternal life is to live with Heavenly Father and Jesus again after we die and are resurrected. Here are five things we can do to gain eternal life:

1. *Keep the Commandments.* When our first parents, Adam and Eve, lived on the earth, they were taught the commandments. Later, Jesus Christ revealed His commandments through the prophets. He even came to earth to show us how to live the commandments perfectly. As we attend church, read the scriptures, have family home evening, and study the gospel, Heavenly Father blesses us for our obedience (see Proverbs 4:4). One wonderful blessing we receive when we choose the right is having the Holy Ghost to guide us. When we choose the right, we stay on the strait and narrow path that leads us back to heaven. If we make a mistake, we must repent and get back on the path. The journey will be hard at times, but it is worth it.

2. *Endure to the End.* As we keep trying to obey the Lord's commandments, we are enduring to the end. If we do this, we can inherit the celestial kingdom, the highest kingdom, where Heavenly Father and Jesus live (D&C 76:92). We can do this if we abide by Their law (D&C 88:22).

3. *Believe in Jesus Christ.* Read 2 Nephi 25:23 (we are saved by grace "after all we can do") and 2 Nephi 25:28 ("deny Him not").

4. *Be Spiritually Minded.* Read 2 Nephi 9:39. If we have righteous thoughts and perform righteous actions, we can obtain the celestial kingdom.

5. *Be Married in the Temple.* In the temple, a husband and wife can be married for eternity, not to be separated by death. Their children can be sealed to them so they can be a family forever. There is no other place on earth where a person can obtain such blessings. Living the gospel helps prepare us to enter this sacred place.

*ACTIVITY

Do *Word Find* to locate phrases that help us obtain the celestial kingdom. Phrases can go any direction and can turn corners. For younger children, circle the first letter of each phrase as a hint.

CHALLENGE

Name reasons why you and your family want to obtain the celestial kingdom and be together forever.

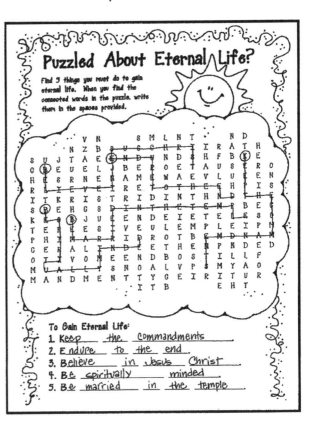

Puzzled About Eternal Life?

Find 5 things you must do to gain eternal life. When you find the connected words in the puzzle, write them in the spaces provided.

To Gain Eternal Life:
1. Keep the commandments
2. Endure to the end
3. Believe in Jesus Christ
4. Be spiritually minded
5. Be married in the temple

TREATS

Eternal Life Rope. Tie thin licorice rope pieces together into five knots/ties, making a large ring. Place a ring around each person's neck, and while pointing to the five knots, talk about the five ways we can prepare to gain eternal life (above). Eternal life is "tied" directly to the gospel of Jesus Christ (see #5 above). If we follow the guidelines, we can create family ties that last forever.

MORE LESSON IDEAS: See *Young Women Manual 3*, lesson 15.

#50
FAMILIES CAN BE TOGETHER FOREVER

AHEAD OF TIME: Print *Temple Eternity Wheel** (shown) using CD-ROM—codes: 50a and 50b (b&w), or 50aC and 50bC (color). To make, cut out wheel parts A and B, punch a hole in the center of each part, and place a paper fastener in center to attach; turn wheel.

SONGS & SCRIPTURE
Sing "I Love to See the Temple" and "Families Can Be Together Forever" (*Children's Songbook,* 95, 188); read D&C 138:47–48 and Mark 10:9.

SHORT LESSON
In the temple, worthy families can be sealed together forever. Even people who died before being sealed in the temple can have these blessings, because temple work is also done for the dead. James E. Faust said, "Temple blessings seal husband and wife together, not only for this life but for eternity. Children and posterity can be linked together by this sealing" ("The Light in Their Eyes," *Ensign,* November, 2005). Without our families, heaven would not be heaven.

Jesus Christ directed the Prophet Joseph Smith to restore the gospel to the earth in these latter days. With the fulness of the gospel on the earth, we can partake of temple ordinances (D&C 124:40–41). The priesthood was restored to the earth so that worthy men can perform sacred ordinances. These ordinances include sealing husband, wife, and children for eternity. (See Matthew 16:19.)

President David O. McKay said, "The marriage ceremony, when sealed by the authority of the Holy Priesthood, endures, as do family relationships, throughout time and all eternity" ("Marriage and Divorce," *Conference Report,* April 1945). Family relationships can last for eternity.

*ACTIVITY

Turn the *Temple Eternity Wheel* to show how families can be together forever.

1. *Pay Tithing.* Keep the windows of heaven open (3 Nephi 24:10) by paying tithing.
2. *Attend Church.* The Lord has commanded us to attend church and "offer up [our] sacraments" on His Sabbath day (D&C 59:9).
3. *Be Honest.* We must be honest with the Lord, other people, and ourselves. Pay an honest tithing, and if employed, do an honest day's work. True integrity is to live honestly all the time, even when no one is around. Honesty is a sign of good character.
4. *Obey the Word of Wisdom.* As we live the Lord's law of health, we can be healthy and obtain "wisdom and great treasures of knowledge; even hidden treasures" (D&C 89:19).
5. *Obey the Commandments.* As we obey we will prosper (see Mosiah 2:22).
6. *Be Married in the Temple for Eternity.* If we are married in the temple, we can gain exaltation. (See D&C 132:19.)

CHALLENGE

Take a walk around the grounds of the nearest temple, or look at pictures of temples. Read about the different temples and the work done there that makes it possible for families to be together forever. (Photos of and articles about the temple can be found in various issues of the *Ensign, New Era,* and *Friend.*) Share your testimony of temple work and how you feel about eternal families.

TREATS

Eternity-circle Cake Doughnuts. Serve cake doughnuts to represent eternal marriage, which has no end and lasts forever if husband and wife obey Heavenly Father's commandments and keep their covenants.

MORE LESSON IDEAS: See *Primary CTR-B Manual 3,* lesson 35.

LIVE WORTHY TO GO TO THE TEMPLE &
DO MY PART TO HAVE AN ETERNAL FAMILY

#51
PREPARE FOR THE TEMPLE

> ***Ahead of Time:*** Print *Temple Prep Puzzle** (shown) using
> CD-ROM—codes: 51 (b&w) or 51C (color).

SONGS & SCRIPTURE

Sing "I Love to See the Temple" and "I Will Follow God's Plan" (*Children's Songbook,* 95, 164); read 1 Nephi 3:7.

SHORT LESSON

Living the commandments helps prepare us to attend the temple, where we can be sealed to our families so we can live with them forever. We will be happy living for eternity with our parents, siblings, and other loved ones, as well as our own spouse, children, and grandchildren. (Explain that if parents have been sealed in the temple before children are born, children are automatically sealed to the parents at birth.)

There are three kingdoms or degrees of glory. To obtain the highest or celestial kingdom, we must receive our endowment (gift from God) in the temple. To achieve the highest degree in the celestial kingdom, we must enter into the new and everlasting covenant of marriage. If we do not, we cannot have increase (children) in the world to come. (See D&C 131:1–4.)

There are seven things we can do to prepare to enter the temple:
1. *Keep the Commandments.* Elder L. Tom Perry explained that because there are now so many temples scattered across the earth, more Church members have the opportunity to receive temple ordinances. Worthy individuals can enter the temple and receive great spiritual blessings as they faithfully keep the promises made there and return often (see "Building a Community of Saints," *Ensign,* May 2001).
2. *Search the Scriptures.* Studying the scriptures will help you develop a testimony of the gospel and help you stay close to the Lord. The Holy Ghost will testify of the truth of what you read (Moroni 10:4–5).

101

3. *Gain a Testimony of the Savior* (see John 4:14–15).

4. *Be Faithful in the Testimony of Jesus.* One who was faithful to the end was the prophet Abinadi. Even when he was about to be burned at the hands of the wicked King Noah, he did not deny his testimony (Mosiah 13:79).

5. *Live the Law of Chastity.* Our body is a temple and is sacred (1 Corinthians 3:16–17; 6:19), and we must keep it that way. No private parts of the body should be shown or touched outside of the bonds of marriage.

6. *Talk to Those Who Have Been through the Temple.* Those who have been endowed have made covenants that are too sacred to discuss outside the temple. But they can share their testimony of the divine work.

7. *Choose a Worthy Companion.* Choosing good friends now can help you choose a righteous spouse later. Make choices that will allow you to be worthy of the kind of person you want to marry someday.

*ACTIVITY

Complete *Temple Prep Puzzle* (shown).

CHALLENGE

Make a personal checklist of things you want to do to become temple worthy. Really challenge yourself to gradually improve until you feel you are temple worthy.

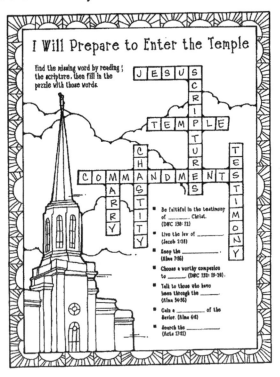

TREATS

Temple Mint Brownies. Make brownies using your favorite brownie recipe or mix. Then frost with mint frosting. Tell family we are "mint" to be together forever through the Lord's plan and temple sealings.

MORE LESSON IDEAS: See *Young Women Manual 3,* lesson 17.

#52
ETERNAL MARRIAGE & FAMILIES

AHEAD OF TIME: Print *Earthly and Eternal Marriage Quiz* puzzles* (shown) using CD-ROM—codes: 52a and 52b (b&w), or 52aC1 and 52bC1 or 52aC2 and 52bC2 (color). To make, cut out both puzzles.

SONGS & SCRIPTURE

Sing "I Love to See the Temple" and "Families Can Be Together Forever" (*Children's Songbook,* 95, 188); read Alma 37:35.

SHORT LESSON

A temple marriage is important and is different from being married outside the temple. A temple wedding is a sacred ceremony where the bride and groom are sealed together for eternity. In this ceremony, the bride and groom make sacred covenants with the Lord. People married outside the temple are married for their lives on earth only.

The Lord teaches that a non-temple marriage ceremony is "not by me nor by my word," but a temple marriage ceremony is "by my word, which is my law, and by the new and everlasting covenant, and it is sealed unto them by the Holy Spirit of promise" (D&C 132:15, 18–19).

A husband and wife who have shared the joys of marriage here on earth will want the same blessings after they are separated by death. Boyd K. Packer taught that with the temple and Heavenly Father's plan of happiness, family relationships can last forever, beyond our mortal lives here on earth. Sacred promises are made in the temple and sacred ordinances performed that offer us the opportunity to return to Heavenly Father and be with our families for eternity. (See "The Standard of Truth Has Been Erected," *Ensign,* Nov. 2003.)

Talk about the reasons why we want to be married in the temple.

*ACTIVITY

The puzzles contain reasons young people give for wanting to marry in the temple, and reasons some do not marry in the temple.

1. For younger children, review puzzles while still together.

2. Mix up puzzle pieces and have family put both puzzles together, reading clues that indicate which puzzle a piece belongs to, e.g., "Each partner can know the other . . . partner is chaste and virtuous."

3. Talk about the difference between the brides' and grooms' smiles and the feelings they may have for the choices they make to marry in the temple or outside the temple.

CHALLENGE

Talk about the reasons why each family member wants the family to be together forever.

TREATS

Temple Cake. Bake a sheet cake and frost it. Cut it into squares and place a candy temple or heart-shaped mints or other candy on top of each square. As children eat the cake, ask them to think of the sweetness they feel as they imagine themselves married for time and eternity to someone they love.

MORE LESSON IDEAS: See *Young Women Manual 1,* lesson 18.

Preview of full-color and ready-to-tear-out-and-use
family home evening and game books and CD-ROMs

Gospel Fun Activities

Fun in a Flash: Gospel Activities

Tons of Fun: Gospel Activities

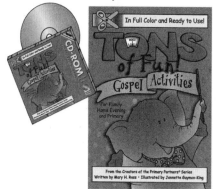

Jesus Loves Me: Gospel Activities

Gospel Games

Funner Than Fun! Gospel Games